The Meaning of Paul for Today

THE
MEANING
OF
PAUL
FOR TODAY

by C. H. DODD

COLLINS ✺ WORLD

A FOUNT BOOK
Published by William Collins+World Publishing Co., Inc.
2080 West 117th Street, Cleveland, Ohio 44111
First Meridian Printing January 1957
Twelfth Printing 1977
ISBN 0-529-02060-2
Library of Congress Catalog Card Number: 57-6677
Printed in the United States of America

PARENTIBUS PRIMITIAS

Contents

. . . But the big courage is the cold-blooded kind, the kind that never lets go even when you're feeling empty inside, and your blood's thin, and there's no kind of fun or profit to be had, and the trouble's not over in an hour or two but lasts for months and years. One of the men here was speaking about that kind, and he called it 'Fortitude.' I reckon fortitude's the biggest thing a man can have—just to go on enduring when there's no guts or heart left in you. Billy had it when he trekked solitary from Garungoze to the Limpopo with fever and a broken arm just to show the Portugooses that he wouldn't be downed by them. But the head man at the job was the Apostle Paul . . ."

Peter Pienaar speaking in *Mr. Standfast*
by JOHN BUCHAN

PREFACE

"These that have turned the world upside down are come hither also." So the people of ancient Salonica judged two men who came proclaiming the Christian Way to a pagan society. By happy fortune, one of the two revolutionaries has survived in his writings, and we are in a position to learn at first-hand how Paul of Tarsus, artisan, scholar, traveller, leader of men, carried out into that imperial world the gospel that had transformed his own life, interpreting it in daring and vivid terms to the mind of his time. A gospel so deeply personal and so widely human can survive the intellectual vicissitudes of centuries, and bear reinterpretation for a new age without losing its vital force.

In this little book I have made some attempt to suggest the place of Paul in the history of religion; but I have been more particularly concerned to bring out what I conceive to be the permanent significance of the apostle's thought, in modern terms, and in relation to the general interests and problems which occupy the mind of our generation. I find in Paul a religious philosophy of life orientated throughout to the idea of a society or commonwealth of God. Such a philosophy finds ready contact with the dominant concerns of our own day.

The basis of this study is the Pauline epistles. There is now a very general agreement among students that in the First Epistle to the Thessalonians, in both epistles to the Corinthians, and in those to the Galatians, Romans, Colossians, to Philemon, and to the Philippians, we possess authentic letters from the hand of the great missionary himself. The order in which they are here named is probably the order of their composition. The remaining five epistles (for no one now supposes that Paul wrote "Hebrews") are still in dispute. Without entering into the dispute here, I may state my belief that the balance of probability is on the side of the genuineness of II Thessalonians and of Ephesians. The latter, however, was probably not written to Ephesus, or at least not exclusively to Ephesus. It may have been some kind of circular letter, written, as we must suppose, almost simultaneously with Colossians. Even if it could be shown not to be from the hand of Paul, it would still remain an important statement of the Pauline philosophy of life in its most developed form. Upon these ten letters I have based my exposition. On the other hand, I cannot persuade myself that the Epistles to Timothy and Titus are, at any rate in their present form, authentic letters of Paul, though they no doubt contain Pauline material. I have not used them as sources for Paul's thought. The Acts of the Apostles, which contain a valuable outline of the Apostle's missionary journeys from the pen of one of his companions, I have treated as only a secondary authority where his inner life and thought are concerned.

I have given quotations from the epistles in an English form which represents my own attempt to reproduce, sometimes by way of paraphrase rather than literal translation, the precise meaning of the original.

They may be compared with any other version that may be accessible. For those who do not read Greek a comparison of a number of different versions is perhaps the next best thing.

I may perhaps be permitted a word upon one aspect of the subject which is at the moment a matter of controversy. The view here taken of the religion from which Paul reacted is very different from the picture of first-century Pharisaism which has recently been set before us by Dr. Abrahams and Dr. C. G. Montefiore. I would observe that Paul himself leaves us in no doubt as to the general effect of the type of Judaism he once professed; and whether or not this type of Judaism was the orthodox Pharisaism of the time, matters little for our present purpose. It is a phase of religion which recurs in many periods, and not only within Judaism. But Paul unequivocally describes himself in his pre-Christian days as a Pharisee. Moreover, we have in the gospels an independent description of Pharisaic religion from a different point of view; and it appears to me that on this matter the gospels and the Pauline epistles explain and corroborate one another. The Jewish scholars I have mentioned have selected from the corpus of Rabbinic writings a set of sayings which give a very attractive picture of Judaism under the Law, and their method of selection seems more critical and discriminating than that pursued by scholars of a former generation —Weber, Schürer, Edersheim—who out of the same corpus produced a far less attractive picture. In any case, however, the evidence for the first century seems to be extracted with difficulty and some uncertainty from a mass of material committed to writing not earlier than the close of the second century. The gospels and the Pauline epistles, on the other hand, are contemporary evidence that in the first century a very strict and exclusive kind of legal puritanism did overshadow the religious life of a group of pious Jews;

that this group was for the time being dominant; and that this group, if not identical with the Pharisees, was at least included in that sect, and largely determined its main religious tendency. Both the gospels and the Pauline epistles give us hints of a more humane and spiritual tendency within Judaism and even within Pharisaism; and this tendency may be represented by the Rabbinic teaching to which Dr. Abrahams and Dr. Montefiore have introduced us. Paul, if Luke has reported him correctly, belonged to "the strictest sect."

To acknowledge my indebtedness to all books and teachers without whose help this little book could never have come into existence would be an endless task; nor is it part of my purpose to give a bibliography. But I cannot refrain from commending to others two books from which I learned very much about Paul: Heinrich Weinel's *S. Paul: the Man and his Work* (E.T. pub. Williams & Norgate 1906), and Adolf Deissmann's *S. Paul: a Study in Social and Religious History* (E.T. pub. Hodder & Stoughton 1912). I could wish that any whom this book may lead to further study of the apostle would read those two books. But above all, let them read the letters themselves—not lections from the letters, but each letter as a unit in itself—either in the original or in a good modern translation such as that of Professor Moffatt.

I am grateful to my colleague Dr. Buchanan Gray, to the Rev. John R. Coates, and to the Editor of this series for suggestions and advice while the book was in proof.

C.H.D.

Mansfield College, Oxford,
July 17, 1920.

The Meaning of Paul for Today

I

FROM JESUS TO PAUL

The story of the Gospels is an unfinished drama. Its historic interest is pivoted upon the conflict between the new liberating message of the Kingdom and the religious system represented by the Pharisees. In the narrative of Mark we watch the forces gather for the inevitable clash. Challenged on one issue after another—with a challenge not forced upon a reluctant situation but growing out of the nature of irreconcilable ideals—the supporters of the old order gradually rally for a battle royal on the whole front of man's religious destiny. More and more it becomes clear that no accommodation is possible. There is a clear issue: on the one hand the Way of the Nazarene, with His startling assertions and denials; on the other hand all that the piety of the time prized as the essentials of a revealed religion. The plot thickens, until in the dim morning light of the fatal Passover the antagonists stand face to face—a nation on one side, the rejected Prophet on the other. The clash comes, and when the earthquake and the eclipse are past, the Established Order remains supreme. The gospel of emancipation has been added to the limbo of shattered illusions, and Pharisaism is triumphant.

That is the crisis of the movement. The situation holds all the elements of real tragedy: a conflict of passionate human interests in which ancient good, becoming uncouth, overcomes the better that might be, and the stirrings of the human spirit after freedom are baffled by historic necessity. But it is evident that the plot is not finished. The whole development has pointed forward, to this situation certainly, but not to this as conclusion. And indeed the gospels themselves obscure the tragedy in a sudden blaze of supernatural light. In the intoxicating joy of Easter morning the defeat is forgotten, and the divine Victor holds the stage. But the faith of the Resurrection is so far a matter of personal religious experience: it is not, as yet, history. As a *dénouement* of the tangled plot it is scarcely even relevant. It is the supreme appearance of the *Deus ex machina*. The risen Christ is Victor indeed over Death; but He is not Victor over the Pharisees. For all the raptures of the disciples, the great system of Pharisaic Judaism stands, as imposing, as self-sufficient, as ever. The tragic conflict is not yet resolved.

Various hands have essayed the construction of a convincing Last Act. For the "realist" school the illusion of the Resurrection is but the deepest note in a final and irredeemable catastrophe. The President of the Immortals has finished His sport with the Nazarene. This is, however, to abandon the data of the plot; for the drama is cast not for disaster but for joy. For the school of romantic melodrama there must be a vindication of poetic justice; and the Risen Christ takes His sword of vengeance and sees His desire upon His enemies. It matters here little whether the *mise en scène* is a Michelangelesque Last Day, or whether, the venue being removed to solid earth, Christ is shown triumphing over the ruins of Jerusalem in the fatal year of Titus's victory.[1] Such a *dé-nouement* is a denial of the central motive of the drama. The character of the Hero must be consistent with itself; and the triumph of a vengeful Messiah is not the triumph of the Victim of Calvary. It is therefore no resolution of the tragic knot.

For a convincing *dénouement* the Hero of the drama—the Speaker of the Sermon on the Mount, the Prisoner of the Sanhedrin, the Bearer of the curse of the Law on Golgotha,—must emerge, He and no other, as the conqueror, the conqueror by His own weapons and by no other, of that unchanged Pharisaism, so noble in its stuff, so pernicious in the final issue of its spirit, which had by an inner necessity of its being destroyed Him. In His victory the Cross must have its indispensable part, and the Resurrection must be shown to be not only an imaginative truth of the supernal world, where the baffled spirit takes refuge from intractable facts, but an active force in real life. Then, and not till then, shall we rest satisfied that the whole dramatic situation has been adequately dealt with and the tragic conflict reconciled.

This is the *dénouement* which History has written. The beginning of it can be told in a few words: "A Hebrew of Hebrews, in regard to the Law a Pharisee . . . I was laid hold of by Christ Jesus . . . I am crucified with Christ, and yet I am alive—not I, but Christ is alive in me." [2] Was revenge ever more complete? Imagine this man (as we may well imagine him, for he was there in spirit at least) among those fanatical Jews who would not enter Pilate's hall "lest they should be defiled," yet stood without clamouring for the death of the Carpenter-Prophet who had dared affront the majesty of their hoary Law. And then see him yielding utterly to the spell of the Cross upon which he or his like had fastened the Rejected. That is real conquest. It is the method of the Christian Revolution.

Here we get the clue to the unity of the New Testament. The Epistles are often opposed to the Gospels
as though they contained "rival philosophies." If in
the story of the Prodigal Son we have the heart of
Christ's message, where, it is asked, is this message to
be found amid the maze of speculation about Law,
Sin, and Sacrifice which fills the pages of the Epistles?
Those who ask that question have failed to notice that
the real problem of that immortal tale is the churl-
ish elder brother. "He was angry and would not go
in"; and in spite of the father's pleadings, there he is
left when the tale ends. Good reason for this: when
Jesus told the tale the elder brothers were fiercely re-
fusing His invitations to renew fellowship with those
despised prodigals whom Jesus "came to seek and to
save." The epistles of Paul show us the elder brother
broken down by the Father's love and leaving home
and its secure delights to go into far countries and
seek out those brothers who still lingered among the
swine and the husks. If the language in which he tells
us how it came about is tortuous and difficult, we may
find in it a sign of the contortions of the spirit which
had to be straightened out before the elder brother
could put away his pride and prejudice and learn his
Father's mind.

In all this we are thinking of Paul not as an individual merely, but as the one mind through which we
can read from the inside what Christ's victorious assault on Pharisaism meant. Paul's letters reflect his
experience; and his experience was an epitome of the
revolution which Christ wrought in religion. There
was in Jewish religion a rich spiritual treasure, gathered through centuries of a history as strange as any
this world can show. But the treasure was not available for mankind, and the process which denied it to
the world made it useless or worse to its possessors.
"You Pharisees," said Jesus, "have taken away the
key of knowledge; you have not entered in yourselves,

and you hindered those who were trying to enter in."
The task which He set Himself was not simply to teach
new truth and leave it at that. He embraced the destiny of Messiahship. That meant a harder task. It
meant gathering up the threads of the past and weav-
ing them into the new design. He came, "not to destroy, but to fulfil." In particular it meant that He
undertook the task of liberating the spiritual treasure
of Israel's faith for humanity. Because He was faithful to that destiny He died on a Roman cross.[3] In
Paul and in the work of his mission we see the task being accomplished. In Paul the devout passion for conduct which distinguished the Jewish religion is seen
liberated, enlightened, made spiritual and personal,
by what Paul found in Christ; and then impressed
upon the life and thought of the wide world in terms
which belong to that strangely composite state of mind
where the mystical East met the Roman West through
the humanizing medium of the great Hellenic tradition.

Because of this Paul is a great figure in the history
of religion. Yet his thought has more than a merely
historic interest. Religion is one of the determining
factors in all history. Too often its organization becomes, as it had become in the time of Christ, an ob-
stacle to the free progress of man. For this reason the
reformer and the revolutionary are very ready to lose
patience with religion and set it aside. Yet the dyna-
mic of religion remains, for good or ill, the strongest
of all human motives. Part of the work of Christ was
that He redeemed religion itself for the saving of
men. It is this side of His work which so powerfully
affected Paul that he remains the classic exponent of
the idea of freedom and universality in religion.
While religion remains the problem, the peril, but also
the one hope of human progress, his work has a contemporary interest.

II

A CITIZEN OF NO MEAN CITY

In the first century of our era Western civilization was coterminous with the Roman Empire. Augustus had set forward with some differences and with greater success the far-reaching policy of his brilliant uncle. He put an end to the evil political system, or want of system, which had made the Roman Republic in its later phases a menace to civilization. The constitution which he established worked at least in the direction of public order and peace. A tendency set in to make the provinces co-operative parts of a great commonwealth instead of the plunder of a narrow-circle of aristocratic families.

Throughout the eastern provinces of the Empire Rome was the inheritor, and in a great measure the upholder, of an earlier system. From the time of Alexander the Great the countries bordering the Levant had come strongly within the circle of Greek civilization. The Greek language was current in most of the towns, even if native languages subsisted alongside them, as they did more especially in the country districts. The towns which had been founded, or transformed, by Greek monarchs in the period after Alex-

ander possessed, and retained under Roman rule, a
limited local autonomy which was the shadow of the
proud independence of the old Greek city-state,
though the encroachments of the central authority
slowly sapped their vitality. In our period, however,
this disintegrating process was not far advanced; and
on the other hand the frequent elevation of these
towns to full municipal rank, carrying with it the Roman citizenship for the municipal aristocracy, gave a
very secure position to the city-state within the Empire. In these municipal communities the old keen intellectual life of Greece, fertilized by its new association with Oriental thought, flourished exceedingly.
Alexandria, Ephesus, Antioch, and many other cities,
had their schools of philosophy; but not only so:
philosophy had come out of the schools, and was rapidly becoming a concern of the man in the street, who
listened with at least that measure of interest which
fashion decreed to the "preaching friars" of the Cynic
or Stoic doctrines. His understanding of them might
be exceedingly superficial, and he might listen only to
find subjects for after-dinner talk; but at least he
was not hopelessly at sea when he heard a philosophic
term used in conversation. There was a large reading
public, and books of a sort were plentiful and fairly
cheap. Not philosophy alone, however, but religion
too, was becoming a popular concern. Alongside the
stately public rituals of the various cities were the
more or less private and independent religious brotherhoods which tried to provide a religious atmosphere
more fervent and more satisfying to the feelings of the
ordinary man than those antiquated and formal rites
could supply.

There was one very widely spread religion which
combined the splendour of antiquity, the tenacity of a
national faith, and the direct personal appeal of a
religion of heart and life—the religion of the Jews.
This strange people was already becoming cosmopoli-

tan. Few towns of any size throughout the Eastern
provinces of the Empire were without their Jewish
colonies. In some of the greatest the Ghetto was an
element of extreme significance in the corporate life
of the place. The Jews had already embarked on that
career for which they seem so singularly endowed by
nature—the career of finance.[1] Their eminence in this
walk of life, together with their fanatical nationalism
and their queer religious customs, made them far
from popular. Yet the attraction of Judaism was
strongly felt, especially in those circles where men
could not find satisfaction with the State religions. The
Jewish communities, or synagogues—civil and religious brotherhoods enjoying much liberty of self-government—were almost everywhere a nucleus for a
more or less loosely knit group of "God-fearers," to
use the Jewish term, who adopted many of the beliefs
and practices of their Hebrew neighbours without actually becoming Jews.

The ancient city of Tarsus in Cilicia is a favourable
example of the municipal city-state; Oriental in the
background of its life and traditions, markedly Greek
in its culture, and enjoying a secure position in the
general order of the Empire. It had its school of philosophy, in which a succession of able teachers had given
a pre-eminence to the Stoic sect. Its commerce pros-
pered. Doubtless the important Jewish colony was intimately associated with this side of the city's life.
Among them was at least one family possessed of the
Roman citizenship, which implies, probably, membership of the order from which the local magistrates
were drawn, and at any rate some social standing
in the town. It is with a son of this family that we
have to do.[2] The boy had the old Hebrew name of
Sha'ul, famous in history as the name of the first King
of Israel, whose tribe, that of Benjamin, was also that
of these Tarsian Jews. That, however, was only his
home-name. To his fellow-citizens outside the syna-

gogue he was Paulus. He must, of course, have possessed a Roman family name and first name—we may
think of him as Gaius Julius Paulus, or Gnaeus Pom-
peius Paulus, if we wish to fit him into his natural
environment in the city of his birth. He learned to
speak and write Greek with ease. He could quote
Greek poets, and use the popular philosophical language of the time easily and naturally. With all this,
however, he was by no means a Greek. His family belonged to the Puritans of Judaism—nationalist in outlook, strict in religious observance. They spoke
Aramaic at home, even though they used Greek at
market or in the City Councilchamber.[3] The boy was,
in fact, sent to Jerusalem, the national capital, in
order that his education should be strong on the dis-
tinctively Jewish side. He made great strides in his
studies, and was probably preparing for the career of a
Rabbi, when events occurred which disturbed the
tenor of his life.[4]

A new sect had appeared within Judaism. It was
composed of the followers of a Galilæan craftsman,
who without any apparent authority had set up for a
Rabbi, and had scandalized the religious leaders by his
bold appeal to the common people and his intensely
critical attitude to the Law and the Temple. He had
fallen into their hands, and they had secured his condemnation at the hands of the Roman Governor on
the charge of being a claimant to the throne of Judæa
—a preposterous charge which nevertheless seemed to
have some foundation in his well-attested claim to
be the "Messiah." The execution had not fulfilled its
purpose to any considerable extent; for the followers
of the Galilæan asserted that he was still alive, and
apparently got people to believe this extraordinary
statement; for the sect was growing with alarming
rapidity. The young Paul saw here a vocation which
commanded his ardent devotion. He would be the instrument of the God of his fathers in putting down

this pestilent and blasphemous heresy. After some very effective work to this end in the city and its neighbourhood, he obtained a commission from the religious authorities to extend the good work. He set out for Damascus with instructions to the local synagogue there to accept his direction in rooting out the Galilæans.[5]

On the way something happened. Paul arrived at the city of Damascus in sorry plight—nervously shaken and half blind. As he recovered, instead of carrying out his commission he commenced a vigorous campaign on behalf of the faith he had set out to destroy.[6] From this time on his whole life was given to the propagation of Christianity. His activities were by no means always pleasing to the older Christians, and especially to their leaders, but after a time he succeeded in establishing some sort of a concordat with the principal men of the Christian community at Jerusalem, which left him a free hand in his mission to the populations of the Roman provinces outside Judæa, including the non-Jewish elements in those populations.[7] Indeed, as time went on, the non-Jewish elements in the Christian communities he founded greatly preponderated over the Jewish, and the type of Christianity which prevailed among them was of a broader, more cosmopolitan type than that of the original community. It was above all a religion of emancipation. "For liberty you were called," is the watchword of Paul's great controversy. This liberty rested upon a personal and inward relation to Christ, replacing allegiance to laws and traditional institutions. The person of Christ was thus not less, but possibly more, central to the new Christians than even to the first preachers of the faith; and Paul's mission was an assertion of the completeness and independence of the Christian faith. It meant that the new religion had broken through the narrow limits of a mere Jewish sect, and set out to claim the world. Paul, Roman citizen as he was, would seem to have conceived the idea—a wild idea it may well have appeared—of "the Empire for Christ." In pursuit of it he spent years in travelling up and down the Roman ways which had linked up the world of that age in so wonderful a fashion, and in navigating the Eastern Mediterranean in storm and shine.

It was an adventurous life he led—and a perilous. Robbers still haunted, in spite of Rome, the inland regions of Asia Minor; and the fleet which had swept the Levant of pirates could not control the Levantine storms, which at least four times brought the intrepid traveller to shipwreck, and once tossed him for twenty-four hours in open sea before rescue arrived. In addition there were the perils to which the propagator of unpopular doctrines exposes himself, even in an age so tolerant on the whole as the first century. It was no doubt something of a joke among Paul's friends that he had once outwitted his enemies by escaping from Damascus in a basket let down from a window, but it was no joke that he was three times scourged by local magistrates (in spite of his Roman citizenship), and no less than five times received the savage maximum penalty of "forty stripes save one" from the Jewish synagogue authorities. This penalty, it is said, was usually commuted or reduced on grounds of mere humanity, and the fact that Paul underwent it five times gives us a hint of the great physical strength which he must have possessed, in spite of his insignificant appearance and his recurrent attacks of a complaint which may have been malarial.[8]

Of his earlier preaching tours we have only the most meagre accounts. Later the record, partly in the form of a diary made at the time, which is generally attributed to his medical attendant Luke, is much more complete. We can trace his strategy. He would settle down in some central spot, preferably a Roman *con-*

ventus or assize town, such as Ephesus, Philippi, or Corinth. Very often he found a favourable starting-point in the local synagogue; and if the doors of the synagogue were closed to him when it was discovered how revolutionary his teaching really was, at least he had by that time made good his footing among the "God-fearer." Sometimes he spoke quite publicly, like the Cynic preachers, in the market-places. At Ephesus he hired a philosopher's lecture-hall after the morning session was over, and gave instruction there daily from 11 to 4.[9] Meanwhile he supported himself by his trade of tentmaking. At Corinth his trade was the means of winning him a footing among the Jews of the place, and of gaining for him one of his most permanent friendships. He found work with a Jew from the Black Sea and his wife, who apparently were in a somewhat large way in the tent-manufacturing business, and travelled between Rome and Ephesus. Prisca and Aquila (the lady is almost always mentioned first) became his trusted coadjutors in the mission; and the incident may suggest to us how the very mobile conditions of international trade and industry in that period lent themselves to the spread of new ideas.[10]

After preaching came the organization of the new Christians into communities, formed partly on the model of the Jewish synagogue with its traditions of self-government, and partly on the lines of the guilds and brotherhoods, which were so popular among the middle and lower classes of the Empire. The actual amount of organization was kept to a minimum, and free cooperation was the central idea. The members of these communities were mainly obscure persons, many of them poor persons, slaves or freedmen, some of them in business, or holding positions under the municipalities, or even in the imperial Civil Service. A few, but not many, persons of wealth; a few, but not many, highly educated persons, might be found in close fellowship with their poorer neighbours in the brotherhood of the Christian Church.[11]

With these scattered communities Paul kept in constant touch, partly through his own and his friends' continual travels, and partly by correspondence, of which we possess some valuable specimens. These letters are for the most part called forth by circumstances. They do not set out to be "literature," but to meet the occasion. One of them is a brief note to a personal friend, about a slave who had run away. Most of the others discuss matters of interest to the particular churches addressed. Two only, those to the Romans and to the Ephesians, make any attempt at a systematic and comprehensive statement of a line of thought. It is from these fragmentary materials that we have to reconstruct Paul's ideas. It is obvious that we cannot hope in such circumstances to attain great completeness or precision. But while there are disadvantages in possessing our materials in this casual form, there are advantages which more than compensate. The letters of Paul are intensely alive —alive as few documents are alive which have come down to us from so remote antiquity. They give us, not a mere scheme of thought, but a living man. We have the same intimate knowledge of Paul that we have, also through his letters, of Cicero, and of scarcely anyone else in those times.

He was a person of extraordinary versatility and variety. He was an enthusiast and a mystic, with powers of rapt contemplation beyond the common. He was also one who could apply the cold criticism of reason to his own dreams, and assess soberly the true value of the more abnormal phenomena of religion. This combination of enthusiasm with sanity is one of his most eminent marks of greatness. His thought is strong and soaring, adventurous rather than systematic. He had a hospitable mind, and a faculty for assimilating and using the ideas of others which is a great asset to anyone who has a new message to propagate: he could think in other people's terms. In it all he was dominated by a white-hot zeal for the truth of which he was convinced as he was convinced of his own existence; and more, by a personal devotion to "the Lord Jesus," as he habitually called the divine Person who, as he believed, had spoken to him first on the road to Damascus and never again left his side. That devotion was his religion, and it controlled his thought and his life. With this went a strong humanity, and a longing that others should enter into the free and joyous life that he had found. This longing was not the mere fervour of the religious bigot for his own creed. It was the passion of a man who loved men and had a genius for friendship. His was a warmly emotional nature, passionate in affection, passionate also in opposition when his hostility was aroused. He said and wrote things he was sorry for, when he wrote or spoke in heat; but it was always a generous heat, kindled by no selfish feelings. The most difficult lesson he had to learn from his Lord was that of tolerance and charity. We can see him again and again in his letters pulling the rein upon his passion lest it get out of control. It was perhaps partly a sense of the need to cultivate tolerance, partly a sense of strategy, which led him at times into ways of accommodation which were easily misunderstood, not only, perhaps, by opponents. He may have made mistakes in this direction, but we can hardly respect too highly the efforts of this naturally intolerant man to "become all things to all men"—to go to the very verge of compromise, and to risk misunderstanding, that he might assert the central and essential principle over against relatively unimportant accidents. That he was able to do so was the result of a sympathy—sufficiently rare in strong, self-confident natures—which could see very clearly the other man's point of view. This faculty sometimes makes difficulties for Paul's interpreters! To these qualities it is hardly necessary to add, so patent is it, that this man displayed an inflexible determination, a persistence that nothing could weary, and a courage that was not a mere constitutional audacity, but a steady fortitude prepared for anything except retreat.[12]

He fell a victim to the malice of his old associates, who could not forgive him for becoming the leader in a movement which had shaken their position to its foundations. On a visit to Jerusalem he was set upon by a mob, and rescued by the Roman officer in command of the garrison. The Jewish authorities preferred charges against him which he offered to answer, as was his privilege, before the Emperor's tribunal. The result of the appeal was that he attained, in strange fashion, his lifelong ambition of visiting Rome.[13] During a long imprisonment he continued his activities, both by intercourse with a wide circle in the City, and by a lively correspondence, which contains some of the most mature fruits of his thought. Towards the end, however, he found himself almost forsaken, and it was a lonely man whom we see dimly through the mists of tradition led to the Three Fountains by the Ostian Way to receive the swordstroke which was his last prerogative as a Roman. His tomb is beneath "St. Paul's without the Walls"; and in spite of the mighty impression he made in his own day, in spite of the veneration of his name, for the bulk of the Christian Church this passionate champion of a religion free, personal, and ethical remains "outside the walls." [14] It is for those who can never satisfy themselves with institutional or legal religion that he has in every age a message.

III

THE HOPE OF THE WORLD

How did the first great Christian missionary look upon the world he lived in, its condition and destiny? Paul has been regarded as a pessimist, and if optimism means the belief that this world as it stands is the best of all possible worlds, then it is difficult to clear him of the charge. He found the world deeply marked with failure and imperfection; but he never dreamed that it need remain so, or that it could ultimately remain so.[1] The whole universe, he says, is groaning and travailing in pain. It is full of suffering and it is a slave to decay—"subject to vanity." That word, echoing the haunting refrain of Ecclesiastes, the classic of pessimism, accurately calls up those suggestions of tiresome futility which the world of nature with its ceaseless round of change and decay brought to the mind of Paul as of many other observers, especially in the East. Man too is part of nature, and shares its heritage of pain and thwarted endeavour. "They were born; they were wretched; they died." So in an Eastern tale the Wise Man sums up the course of human history. So far the outlook of Paul does agree with the typical Oriental pessimism.

But for him that is not the whole story. Beside the groaning and travailing there is in the world an "eager expectation." The whole universe, with head outstretched and intense gaze, is waiting for something very glorious which shall finally deliver it from slavery to futility and give a meaning to all its pangs. It is a sorry world, but an expectant world, subject to vanity but saved in hope; travailing now, but destined to glory. It is a world, above all, with a real history; and that is what Oriental pessimism never allows. But the conception of a universe in which there is real movement and real development is very congenial to the modern mind. Indeed, we feel ourselves here very much at one with Paul in his view of the world. We, like him, dare not deny the miserable facts of pain and failure, in nature and in man as part of nature; but we would fain believe that the change and flux have a tendency, and that tendency an upward one. That the upward tendency is automatic and inevitable we are perhaps less sure than our fathers. Perhaps we feel, like Paul, that the universe—or at least this earth —is waiting for something. And perhaps, too, Paul was right in thinking that the key to its destiny was in the hand of man.

For us, even more definitely than for him, man is part of nature. In man the energy of the material world, the instinct of animal life, rises—precariously and incompletely, but really—into the sphere of consciousness and of will. In him the apparently blind impulse towards greater perfection working, as we believe, in the universe, attains a measure of freedom and self-direction. In him also instinct, become rational, can turn back upon the material world out of which he has partly emerged and actually control its changes, aid its advance, intercept its decay. Directly upon his body, indirectly upon other parts of the physical universe, the thought of man, and the action which is the outcome of his thought, works beneficently or destructively according to his choice. For the most part his action upon the world seems blundering and of doubtful value. The immense control of manner that man has gained—our so-called "progress"—is of very uncertain benefit to the universe conceived as a system aiming at perfection in every part after its kind. But if man himself could be different; if his own life were altered by the attainment of right relations with God and with his fellow-man, his role in the world in which he lives might be a more beneficent one than we can well imagine. The artist uses the material world as means to the expression of that love of beauty which is one aspect of the love of God, and thereby transfigures the material—delivers it, as Paul might say, from the bondage of decay into the liberty of glory. If we could all become artists over the whole of life, using our whole environment to express the highest spiritual relations within our reach, is it not possible that the influence of humanity upon the world might change its whole aspect? Paul at least thought that in some way the universe was waiting for man to attain right relations in the spiritual sphere —"waiting for the revealing of the sons of God."

A contemporary poem addresses "Everyman" in language which beautifully suggests a thought akin to Paul's[2]:

> All things search until they find
> God through the gateway of thy mind.
>
> Highest star and humblest clod
> Turn home through thee to God.
>
> When thou rejoicest in the rose
> Blissful from earth to heaven she goes;
>
> Upon thy bosom summer seas
> Escape from their captivities;
>
> Within thy sleep the sightless eyes
> Of night revisage Paradise:

In thy soft awe yon mountain high
To his creator draweth nigh;

This lonely tarn, reflecting thee,
Returneth to eternity;

And thus in thee the circuit vast
Is rounded and complete at last,

And at last, through thee revealed
To God, what time and space concealed.

How Paul conceived the "emancipation" of the physical world we cannot tell. Many contemporary thinkers imagined a miraculous change of the very substance of things—a new heaven and a new earth in strict literalness. Paul may have shared the belief. But the important point seems to be that he conceived such a change as no accident, but directly connected with the working out of human relations. In attacking what was wrong with men he firmly believed that he was attacking the problem of the universe. Shall we put it in this way, that the problem of reality is at bottom a problem of personal relations? [3] No purely physical speculations will ever solve for us the problem of this tangled universe. Personality holds the clue; and the solution is personal and practical. The spiritual aspirations of man, faithfully followed, let us into the secret of evolution and give the only hint we can get of its purposes.

We turn, then, from the Apostle's philosophy of the world to his philosophy of human history. We shall expect to find it based upon a gloomy estimate of human life as it is, saved from pessimism by a tremendous faith in what it may become. He saw the world of men in two opposing groups—his own nation and pagan society, i.e. practically the pagan Græco-Roman Empire. His interest in that Empire, its ethical and social life and problems, was intense. It dated, doubtless, not from his conversion to Christian-

ity, but from his youth at Tarsus. Only the character
of that interest was changed from condemnation and
despair to hope when he looked afresh with the eyes
of Christ. The Empire indeed, as he saw it, was rot-
ten with vice and injustice. His picture of pagan
morals in the opening chapter of the Epistle to the
Romans is lurid, but most of it could be corroborated
from pagan sources. His judgment, however, was
not undiscriminating or blind. Even in the pagan he
recognized a natural knowledge of God, a conscience
bearing witness to a "law written on the heart," an
instinctive knowledge of right and wrong.[4] Its political system, he confessed, aimed at the vindication of
right and the suppression of wrong, and in its measure succeeded.[5] Its imperial law restrained the threat-
ened outbreak of undiluted and anarchic evil.[6] And
yet he saw a monstrous perversion of the whole. A
mass of humanity, the offspring of God, had somehow
taken a wrong turn so decisive that at every step it
was farther from God. The light that was in it had
become darkness; and God had given it over to its
own unrestrained passions.

It is in this strain that Paul inveighs in his letter to
Rome against the corruption of the Pagan world; and
so far, we can imagine an audience of Pharisaic Jews
listening with applause. Suddenly Paul turns upon
them and drives home the charge that they have known
better but not done better. "You call yourself a Jew,
and rely upon your law, and boast of your God. . . .
You set up for a guide of the blind, a light to the
benighted, a trainer of the ignorant, a teacher of in-
fants. . . . You teach others, but do not teach yourself. You preach 'Do not steal,' and you are a thief!
You preach 'Do not commit adultery,' and you are an
adulterer! You abominate 'idols,' but you plunder
their temples! You, who boast about your law, by
breaking the law dishonour God!" [7] They are strong
words for a Jew to use to Jews. We can surely over-

hear in them the indignant shame of a high-minded
Israelite who found that in the great cities of the pa-
gans men of his own race had made the name of
Jew to stink by their hypocrisy and baseness.

We must not forget that the darkness of this picture is relieved by a pagan here and there who "did by
nature the things of the Law" and by at least a faithful remnant among renegade Israel. But Paul found
nowhere, neither in the pagan world nor yet among
his own people, the moral power and stability which
his sense of the divine holiness demanded of "sons of
God." Out of the mass of weakness and corruption
the universe awaited their revealing: where could they
be found? To the inquiring mind, all history comes to
be a search for the family of God, the Divine Commonwealth through which alone man and the world can
attain emancipation. This Commonwealth of the sons
of God can only be of God's own creation. Thus from
the divine point of view history shows God seeking
His sons among sinful humanity. Paul had inherited
from his Pharisaic training a belief in divine predestination, though the Pharisees, we are told, somehow
managed to preserve alongside of this doctrine a belief in human free will. The use, however, which Paul
makes of the doctrine is most instructive. It is for him
the means of asserting and maintaining the freedom
and originality of God's personal dealings with men.

The Pharisaic God was for practical purposes an
Absentee. He had created the world; at a few points
in the remote past He had definitely intervened; in
the future He would once more intervene in Judgment; but in the present age the history of man was
the mechanical working-out of an inexorable Law.
The pagan mind, on the other hand, was haunted by
fatalism. In that age philosophy tended to support
with its authority the ancient popular superstition
that a man's fate was controlled by his stars. You
were born with a certain horoscope, and by that your

fate was irrevocably fixed. That the dominion of the
"world-rulers," the "elemental spirits," was broken[8]
was a part of the message of primitive Christianity
which scarcely appeals to us; but it came with the
sense of a tremendous relief to the spirit-ridden mind
of the first century, as it still comes to many in China
and India. Over against the mechanical rule of law
and the domination of the fatal star alike, Paul main-
tains that God always and in every age is free to deal
personally with men.[9] He called Abraham to be His
son, but He did not then leave natural heredity to
produce His Divine Commonwealth. He chose
Isaac; He chose Jacob; He called seven thousand in
Elijah's day, who stood firm against the idolatry of
their time; He chose the faithful remnant on whom
Isaiah set his hope—the saving salt of a lost people.
Last of all He ordained as His Son Jesus the son of
David "according to the flesh," and through Him
brought a multitude out of all nations into "adoptive
sonship." [10] At every point a free, personal act of God.

The doctrine of absolute and arbitrary divine
sovereignty which accompanies this view of history
seems to us destructive of human freedom in any
real sense; but in the early preaching of the Gospel
it served a purpose of the highest value. If you could
believe that your destiny was not decided by the working of mechanical law, or determined by a ruthless
fate, but that the divine vocation of which you were
conscious in your own soul was an act of sovereign
power on the part of a God present here and now to
save you, it would surely give a new sense of assurance and stability in the face of all hostile forces. It
is with that intent that Paul always makes use of the
argument from predestination. "Those whom He
foreknew He also predestined; and those whom He
predestined He also called. . . . If God be for us,
who can be against us?" [11] And any philosophy which
admits a divine government of the universe must

leave a place for something like this Pauline theory
of a "selective purpose." [12] As Paul meant it, it is not
a doctrine of determinism, but rather a protest
against the prevalent determinism of his time by the
assertion that a real "fresh start" is possible at any
time where God comes into fresh touch with man.

So much for history viewed from the divine end.
From the human end it is the story of the progressive
response of sons of God to the calling of their Father,
and the resultant constitution of the People of God.
On man's part, simple trust in God gives play to the
divine purpose. The inevitable instance of such trust
in the past was Abraham: "Abraham trusted God,"
Paul quotes more than once.[13] So soon as a man was
found to take that attitude to God, the People of God,
or the Divine Commonwealth, was already in existence, if only in germ. It was maintained and in-
creased, Paul argued, by exactly the same means, by
the successive personal response of men in each generation to the calling of God.[14] Behind all the scholastic arguments of the Epistles to the Romans and the
Galatians lies the crucial question whether religion is
a matter of national inheritance and external tradition, or a matter of ever-fresh personal response to the
gracious dealing of God. In form, the nation founded
by Abraham was the People of God; but "the majority of them God did not choose," as was shown by the
fact that in spite of their participation in the ordi-
nances of the Covenant they "were unfaithful." [15] The
nation possessed the outward forms of a Divine Commonwealth or Kingdom of God or "Theocracy," but
it was only a minority in the heart of it that kept
hold of the reality. Elijah's Seven Thousand, Isaiah's
Remnant—these were the representatives of the true
People of God, the faithful Divine Commonwealth
hidden in the bosom of apostate Israel.[16] Not that
even they could be said to have attained perfect obedience to the precepts of the divine Will, or to be able

to claim God's favour on the basis of their own achievement, but their "faith" in God kept them true, amid doubts, uncertainties, failures, and imperfections, as they waited confidently for the next stage of His dealing. For the time being, this Divine Commonwealth was in "bondage." Like an heir in his minority "under tutors and guardians," it led a kind of provisional existence under the shadow of the Law, unable to win freedom of action or to become a power of salvation to the world.[17]

The upshot of past history, as Paul saw it, may be put in these terms: in the pagan world, a few isolated individuals doing, in some measure, the will of God as revealed in their consciences, but unable to form a real community;[18] in Israel, a Theocracy in form, but so bound and hedged about as to be unable to effect anything for God in the world at large. The prophets had always foreseen that this age must be succeeded by another, in which the free life of the Spirit should create a world-wide society or Kingdom of God. Now with the Resurrection of Christ, Paul held, this new age began. The heir had come of age; the dim light of an ever-deferred hope had given place to the clear dawning of the "The Day." [19] Out of Israel and out of the pagan world alike God was calling His sons into a real community-life through which the world should be saved. This is the "mystery kept silent through agelong periods, but now revealed." [20] A "mystery" to Paul's Greek readers meant a dramatic spectacle which conveyed to those who had the key deep truths of the unseen world unsuspected by the "profane" mind, and not to be expressed in language. Even so the historic drama of Christ's death and resurrection had brought into clear light the hidden purposes of God, by uniting faithful men, out of all nations and classes, in one firm commonwealth free and powerful to do the will of God.

Thus the New Age had begun. That is a fundamental belief of all early Christians. They knew they were living at a crisis—at the crisis—of History. They were "children of The Day"—the day of God's self-revelation; they were inhabitants of a new world.[21] They were quite sure that fresh powers had entered into them, and that the divine purpose was forcing its way through their efforts into the world at large. And though they knew also that the time of crisis must bring sufferings which they must share, of which indeed they must bear the brunt,[22] yet they were upheld and animated by a vivid hope to which nothing seemed too good to be true. That hope clothed itself in strange apocalyptic imagery. Paul, in his earlier letters, and no doubt in his earlier preaching, made free use of this imagery, though it is clear that he was all the time re-interpreting it. At first he certainly expected that before long—at all events in his lifetime —Christ would visibly return and lead His people in an aggressive campaign against all evil;[23] that He would reign over a Kingdom which would come to include those Israelites who in the course of the "selective purpose" had fallen out by the way, and, we may take it, those pagans also who had hitherto remained unrepentant, until the whole race should be gathered into one.[24] At the End of All, having put down all hostile or rival authority and power in heaven and on earth, He would offer us all to God, and God would be all and in all.[25]

Putting aside so far as we can what is (for us at least) merely figurative in this sketch of the future, we can at least see how for Paul the time in which he lived was the turning-point of history; before Christ, the disintegration of humanity, and the gradual selection of a small remnant to carry on God's purpose; from the coming of Christ, the re-integration of the race, the inclusion, step by step, of the "rejected," and the attainment of final unity for all that is, in the perfected Sovereignty or Kingdom of God. As he grew older, the apocalyptic imagery of the earlier days tended to disappear at least from the foreground of his thought, and more and more his mind came to dwell upon the gradual growth and upbuilding of the Divine Commonwealth. He saw the Church going out into the world to save the world, ready to "fill up what was lacking of the sufferings of Christ" for the sake of mankind, and restlessly seeking out the sons of God in the name of their Father. He saw it impelled ever further and further in the quest, constrained by the love of Christ, reconciling, liberating, including in its universal fellowship Jew and Greek, barbarian, Scythian, slave, freeman, and so working out the divine purpose to "sum up all things in Christ." [26] If this is an idealized picture of what the Church has been even at its best, it gives the standard of what it might be, a perpetual rebuke and challenge to a Church which has fallen from its ideal.

IV

THE QUEST OF THE DIVINE COMMONWEALTH

An attempt has been made in the preceding chapter to sketch the philosophy of history which can be discovered in the writings of Paul. In its main outlines it is set forth in his letter to the Christians of Rome. That fact is not without significance. The Epistle to the Romans is the manifesto of Paul's missionary program written at the very height of his activity, in the near prospect of a visit to the imperial centre of the world. For the Romans, as for us, it was necessary to have some understanding of his philosophy of history if they were to appreciate what were his aims and principles in preaching the Christian Gospel throughout the Roman world. The hope of the world, as he saw it, lay in the "revelation of the sons of God"—the realization of the Divine Commonwealth. In his faith in Christ he held the key to the "mystery" of that Divine Commonwealth. He knew the secret of its realization. Hence he was a missionary.

In the circles in which Paul was brought up there was a perfectly definite theory about the Divine Commonwealth. He was a Jew, and the Jews believed themselves to be in the most absolute sense God's chosen people. The divine blessing was an estate entailed upon the historic nation derived, as was believed, from Abraham, and preserved intact through the centuries by its observance of the institutions summed up in the Mosaic Code. The reverence and enthusiasm with which these archaic institutions were regarded are almost inconceivable. That they represented the eternal laws of all reality was held certain. It was said that the Law was the pre-existent plan according to which the world had been created, and that the Deity spent eternity in its study.[1] The purport of such apparently hyperbolic expressions was clearly to identify the particular set of rules for life and thought contained in the Pentateuch with absolute truth and absolute right. With such a belief it is no wonder that those who took it seriously had an outlook upon the world which bears the appearance of national arrogance run to an almost insane extreme. Strangely, and yet intelligibly enough, even the Jew whose personal life and conduct had little resemblance to the high ethical ideals of the Old Testament felt an exaltation of spirit as he thought that his nation alone of all peoples of the earth possessed the inmost secret of things. The rest of mankind was there for Israel's sake[2]—to serve Israel or to chastise Israel as might be Jehovah's inscrutable purpose, but in any case to be subjugated or blotted out in the end, when God should finally declare His judgment. The Jewish people was the Divine Commonwealth.

The Pharisaic party which cherished these views with deepest conviction was by no means indifferent to the fate of the non-Jewish world. It is even probable that this sect was prominent in the vigorous Jewish propaganda which was going forward throughout the Mediterranean area at the time when Christianity appeared. But in the nature of things such propaganda could only be a kind of spiritual imperialism. It rested on the assumption of the inherent and eternal superiority of one nation and one form of culture over all others. Individuals of other nations could be incorporated in the chosen people, but it was only as naturalized aliens that they could take their place. They were held at arm's length, admitted only grudgingly and by degrees to the spiritual privileges of Israel, and they could only be full members of the community by adopting all the peculiar, and in part barbarous, rites and observances of the Jewish religion, including the rite of circumcision, which was counted by Greeks and Romans as a degradation. It was no wonder that the civilized world of the time looked with scorn upon these pretensions, so opposed to the broad humanism of the Stoics with their gospel of Cosmopolis, the City of Zeus. For all that, Judaism had somewhere within it a moral passion and power of regeneration before which even Stoicism was impotent. Many an earnest soul was willing even to bow to the arrogant pretensions of the Jew for the sake of the ethical reality he stood for, so strangely high and pure in spite of the meanness of its earthly vessels.

In such a position of affairs we can see the peril to the future of humanity. It is not good that men should submit themselves to the dictation of any one people, whether in politics or in religion. It is not good that the highest personal morality should be associated with a corporate egotism. All imperialisms are a denial of the fundamental unity of mankind, however bright their fallacious promise of such a unity. The propaganda of Imperialism is a propaganda against the brotherhood of man, and if missions to the "heathen" or to the "lower classes" are inspired by the national or class egotism which believes that "our sort" must be right and everybody else must accept our direction, then they are a form of spiritual imperialism. "Woe to you, scribes and Pharisees, play-actors!" Jesus is reported to have said; "you traverse sea and land to make one convert, and when he is there, you make him twice as much a child of Gehenna as yourselves." [3] It sounds severe, even unfair, but religious propaganda which rests on sectional pride always runs this risk.

Paul the Jew had to suffer the shattering of his deepest beliefs before he came through to a new conception of a missionary's work. He had to learn that there was no distinction of Jew and Gentile. It needs some effort of the imagination to realize what this surrender cost him. Perhaps it was like an American of the South being obliged to admit that he must sit at the feet of the negro, or an Australian asked to view with equanimity, even to further, the spread of "yellow" civilization. As a young man he had heard the humanistic talk of popular Stoicism at Tarsus, and his religious instincts revolted against what seemed an obliteration of profound moral distinctions. Now he must capitulate. The Stoics were right: God had made of one stock all nations on earth.[4] Of all He made the same demands, to all the same offer on the same terms. In the present corruption of the world no one nation could stand aloof and say, "This is the wickedness of other people." If humanity was cursed by sin, *all* had sinned, whether Jew or pagan, and all had missed the divine splendour of ideal humanity.[5] God alone could make good what was amiss, and He could do it only with men who abandoned all self-confidence (all "glorying in the flesh," as our translation of Paul has it). How this new creation was to take place we must presently inquire. For the moment we are concerned to see this man as the pioneer of a new method of establishing the Divine Commonwealth. He saw it growing like a body, cell to cell; or built like a temple, stone to stone, through the sharing of a common life, the surrender to a common purpose. The union of mankind he saw taking place at a

level of common humanity deeper than all the rami-
fications of nationality, culture, sex or status. He
asked only that each should confess his part in the
general wrong, and trust God to put him right in
God's own way—not the way of his preference ("not
my own righteousness, but the righteousness which
comes from God through trusting Him"). On that
common basis he saw a unity growing out of the
very diversity of men's minds and gifts—many members, but one body; diversity of gifts, but one spirit.[6]
On these terms he appealed to the devout Pharisee of
the Jewish synagogue, to the philosophers of Athens,
the civil servants of the Empire at Rome, the traders
of Corinth, the artisans of Ephesus, the slaves and
"riff-raff" of the seaport towns, the half-Greek inhabitants of Asiatic cities, and the barbarians of Malta and
the Lycaonian highlands. With this demand he stood
before kings and proconsuls, and with the same offer
he won the rascal fugitive slave Onesimus, and made
him "a brother beloved."

It has already been indicated that ideas of a universal commonwealth were present in the pagan world.
Rome, largely inspired by the sublime ideals of Stoicism (which in Paul's time gave a Prime Minister to
the Empire, and in the next century ascended the
throne itself), was consciously aiming at its establish-
ment. Paul, himself a Roman, was stirred by the
thought of what Rome was doing. Imperial Rome is
the background of his greatest epistle, and the writing
of it was largely inspired by the thrilling prospect of
setting up the standard of Christ on its ancient Seven
Hills. And yet he knew that Rome must fail. The
Roman Empire could never become the Kingdom of
God. It lacked the moral foundation. Even its philosophic instructors were content to compromise with
institutions which oppressed men and superstitions
which degraded them. The Empire was founded on
violence: Rome "made a solitude and called it

peace." It transcended national boundaries, but it ruled by an upper class of the privileged and showed its contempt for the poor by giving them "bread and circuses." Its blossoming might be the fine flower of humane culture, but its roots were in the degradation of slavery. And it demanded the abject worship of an autocrat, which meant bondage, not of the body alone, but of the spirit. The failure, in the end, of this magnificent attempt to unify the human race justified Paul's judgment on it. He sought its best ends, by means which did not kill but made alive the individual spirit. Rome crushed the individual to glorify the State. In the end it destroyed itself by strangling or crippling every institution of local government and every guild or corporation through which free co-operation was possible. It was characteristic of Paul's mission that wherever he worked there sprang up live, vigorous local communities, free and democratic, where individual initiative was prized and individual gifts found play. Each of these communities felt itself to be a living embodiment of that City of God whose ultimate reality was eternal in the heavens. "Your citizenship is in heaven"—you are a colony of the Divine Commonwealth—Paul wrote to the Christians of the Roman colony of Philippi.[7] This was because in each individual member the great change had taken place whereby the "life of the (New) Age"[8] became a personal experience.

There is nothing which in the last resort can unite mankind but the free contagion of this life. It is a current view today that economic interdependence will unify mankind. It is questionable. Nor indeed can political organization attain that end, as we are learning every day, unless the spirits of men be made one. We see rather a forecast of the true process when the vision of the artist or the rapture of the musician draws men together across the barriers, for they too have touched life at a point deeper than our transient divisions. But there is something deeper and more universal than art or music, and of that Paul speaks. Man is born to be a son of God, and only in "the liberty of the splendour of the sons of God" can the commonwealth of man be founded. The missionary enterprise of Christianity, in its ideal and largely in its practice, is an indication of the true method of building the brotherhood of man in which the Kingdom of God may find expression. When the missionary enterprise enters, as it has sometimes done, into an unnatural alliance with national ascendancies and all the superstitions of Empire, it stultifies itself. But when the missionary goes out, not as a European or an American, but as a Christian simply, a son of God seeking brotherly fellowship with sons of God waiting to be revealed in all nations—when he makes his appeal to the simply human in men, speaking the word of reconciliation which unites us to God and to each other—then he is the truest servant of the coming Kingdom that the world can show. Such was Paul the Missionary.

It was not to be expected that Jewish patriotism would acquiesce in this treason to the national idea. The tradition of privilege was too strong. Even any loftier souls who may have given up the dream of political domination yet clung tenaciously to their spiritual ascendancy. Jerusalem might never become another Rome, but Jerusalem was the only conceivable spiritual metropolis of the world. To them Paul declared that their Jerusalem was a slave city, bound hand and foot to an obsolete tradition: "Jerusalem above is free, which is our Mother!" [9] The unifying patriotism of the City of God—that "city within whose walls the souls of the whole world may assemble" [10]—was in that watchword pitted against the divisive patriotism of the tribal State and tribal religion. That is the inner meaning of the fight which Paul waged all his life against his old associates.

There can be little doubt that in principle the question of "universalism" was decided for Paul in the fact of his conversion, even though it remains highly probable that both his theory of the matter and his practice underwent development. The Christianity with which he had come into direct conflict was not the timid "right wing" which under James the Lord's brother sought a quiet *modus vivendi* with national Judaism, but the militant radical section which the martyred Stephen had led into the most decisive break with the national and legal tradition.[11] It was to this radical Christianity that he was converted. From the beginning he had against him the organized force of the Jerusalem Sanhedrin and the synagogues. The main count in their indictment was that he was a traitor to the Law and a confederate of Gentiles. "It is the Jews," he wrote bitterly from Corinth in the first letter of his that has survived, "who killed the Lord Jesus and the prophets and drove us out, who never obey God, who are the enemies of all mankind, and *who try to prevent us from speaking to the pagans for their salvation.*" [12] The turn of phrase shows how Paul felt about it.

But he had also against him the conservative right wing of the Church, which included some at least of the original disciples, though we may believe that converts from the sect of the Pharisees formed the backbone of the party.[13] So far as the more moderate leaders are concerned, we can understand and respect their position. They were cautious in the presence of an untried venture. They saw, and perhaps report exaggerated, the perils of Paul's bold propaganda. Some of the language he used about freedom from law had a dangerous suggestion of anarchy. They did not know to what subversive doctrines he might commit the Christian movement. Moreover, they felt, and not unreasonably, that they were likely to know the mind of their Master better than this new-comer who had never heard Him speak, and they could not think that He wished the door quite so widely opened. It is not the only time in history that the nearest followers of a great leader have failed to understand his secret, even while they died for his cause.

Nevertheless, Peter, generous and impulsive as ever, had, without thinking much of what was implied, early taken steps in the direction of a liberal attitude to pagans. It was perhaps his influence which led to the concordat under which Paul worked for some time with the concurrence of the "pillars" of the Church at Jerusalem, and according to the Acts of the Apostles it was he who persuaded the Council of Jerusalem to sanction a liberal missionary policy in Syria and Cilicia.[14] And indeed when he visited Paul and his friends at Antioch, he was quite carried away by the enthusiasm of the forward movement. The controversy had come to hinge upon the question of eating at table with converts from paganism who had not been adopted into the community with the recognized Jewish ceremonies, especially circumcision. Large questions do sometimes turn upon small points. This point, however, was not so small as it might seem. It is not a small thing to-day for an Indian Brahmin to break caste by eating with a pariah. Moreover, the Christian brotherhood had from the first made its life centre about the common table. To refuse to break bread with a fellow-Christian was to deny that he had any part in Christ, at whose table the brotherhood met. Peter, however, sat at table with these half-Greek Syrians in the friendliest way, and the difficulty seemed over. Then came members of the extreme "right wing"—adherents of James, but no doubt *plus royalistes que le roi*. Peter, frightened, drew back. Even Paul's old friend and leader, Barnabas, gave way. The dispute culminated in a regrettable public quarrel between Peter and Paul, the echoes of which, perhaps, were to be heard later even in the Pauline churches.[15] Peace, however, seems to have been restored, as between the leaders. Peter and John probably took in the end the liberal view, and even James kept on friendly terms with Paul, and it was not by any ill-will of his, but quite the contrary, that his ill-calculated tactics ultimately contributed to Paul's arrest and imprisonment.[16]

But the extreme conservatives pursued him everywhere with unabated zeal. They opened war by a powerful mission to Galatia, where they all but succeeded in winning to a Judaic Christianity the churches Paul had founded.[17] From that time he had to count "perils from false brethren" among the difficulties of his work.[18] During most of his active life he was a nonconformist and a free-lance, regarded with cool and rather suspicious tolerance by some of the most respected leaders of the Church, and with horror by the "ultra-orthodox" right wing. We need not impugn their motives, as Paul did in the heat of controversy. They were honest men and zealous servants of the Gospel as they understood it. Paul made mistakes, and some bad ones, in the course of the struggle. But Paul was right and his opponents were wrong on the main issue.

It was the controversy with the Jewish National Party in the Church that drove Paul to formulate and defend the principles underlying his Gospel. The laboured argument which fills large sections of the letters to Rome and Galatia—and which has often been treated as almost the only valuable element in the Pauline writings—is to be regarded as apologetic directed against Pharisaic Judaism (which he knew by early training from top to bottom) and its revival within the Christian Church. This apologetic is almost accidental; it does not represent his missionary preaching; it represents the theoretical justification of its principles against those who denied his right so to preach at all in the name of Christ. Much of it is *argumentum ad hominem* and of temporary validity only as addressed to those particular adversaries. The very success he gained antiquated his polemic. But concealed beneath these temporary forms of thought is his permanent contribution to the philosophy of religion. His victory, indeed, was less complete than it seemed. By other channels than that of the Judaistic propaganda the old spirit of Pharisaism entered into the Church: its narrowness, its formalism, its bondage to tradition, its proneness to national and class prejudice. We shall not fight it today, in ourselves or in the Church, with the precise weapons which Paul used; but if we can read his essential thought out of its obsolete forms into the living language of today we shall at least know how to deal with that undying Pharisee whom most of us carry beneath our hats. But, also we shall have learned what Christianity is, from the man who, though he knew not Christ after the flesh, divined better than any what Christ stood and stands for.

V

THE ANCIENT WRONG

We have seen how Paul saw humanity in evil case,
and how he devoted himself to its rescue from this
evil case by "the revealing of the sons of God" as a
closely knit Divine Commonwealth. More precisely,
he saw mankind enslaved, and lived for its emancipation; and he saw it alienated, and lived for its reconciliation. Those are the two great words of the Pauline
gospel: "redemption," "atonement." By this time they
have become wholly theological terms, with their
meaning confused by centuries of dogmatic definition. "Redemption" was the process by which a slave
obtained his freedom. Thousands of Jews taken pris-
oners in the wars had been sold into slavery in the
Roman dominions, and it was a popular work of be-
nevolence for wealthy Jews to "redeem" them into
liberty. That is the source of the metaphor. We shall
therefore do well to use the term "emancipation" as
the nearest equivalent of the Pauline expression.
"Atonement" is an old English word meaning the restoration of unity ("at-one") between persons who are
estranged. In *Richard II* Shakespeare makes the king
say to the rival noblemen, Mowbray and Bolingbroke,

> *"Since we cannot atone you, we shall see*
> *Justice design the victor's chivalry."*

The secondary meanings which the word has acquired
are foreign to the language of Paul. In the Authorized
Version of the New Testament "atonement" is the
translation of a perfectly ordinary Greek word for the
reconciliation of estranged persons. Paul saw men
divided into hostile camps "biting and devouring one
another." [1] Behind that internecine strife he saw the
hostility of men to God their common Father. Get rid
of the enmity toward God, and the divisions of men
may be overcome. "While we were enemies we were
reconciled to God through the death of His Son":
"He is our peace, who made both one, and broke
down that dividing wall, our enmity." [2] "Reconciliation," then, of the estranged, "emancipation" of the
enslaved, are the cardinal points of Paul's Gospel.

We have now to ask, What is the enslaving force,
and what is the cause of the alienation? To those
questions, Paul gives one answer, Sin. That word too,
however, he used in a sense different from that in
which it has come to be used in modern theology and
ethics. To understand his view of sin we must make
our way through some rather tangled metaphysics.

Paul conceived reality in a dualistic way. There are
two planes of being, the one eternal, the other temporal; the one visible, the other invisible.[3] The visible
world is in some sort a revelation of the invisible,
but an imperfect revelation, for it is entangled in a
mesh of decay ("corruption"). Decay is, in fact, so in-
separable a property of the visible world that Paul
gives us no other general term for its material substance. He simply calls it "decay," describing it by its
most evident property rather than defining it. Similarly, he describes the substance, if we may so call it,
of the invisible world as "splendour" ("glory"), and

he may have conceived it, with many Greek thinkers, as akin to light and fire.

The cosmical aspect of the question, however, is
only vaguely touched upon. It is only in man that
Paul shows us anything approaching a complete
scheme of the relations of the two planes. For man
belongs, at least potentially, to both. His bodily existence partakes of the nature of the temporal and visible: "he wears the image of the earthy." In him the
visible substance is "flesh," material, and inevitably
subject to decay. The flesh is temporarily animated
by the *psyché* (if we use the word "soul" we are suggesting false implications), which is the principle of
conscious life, including even intellectual processes,
but not belonging to the heavenly or eternal order. On
the other hand is the "inner man," whose nature is
different. About the inner man in the non-Christian,
Paul is somewhat vague; but it appears that the
"reason" by which God is known to all men, and the
"heart" upon which His law is written, partake of
the nature of the invisible and eternal world.[4] The
non-Christian is, however, to Paul's mind an imperfect,
immature specimen of Man. It is in the Christian that
we must study human nature in its developed form.
Here the inner man is definitely described as "spirit"
(*pneuma* as distinct from *psyché*). Like "flesh,"
spirit is a *continuum*; it is the form of being of God
Himself and of the risen and glorified Christ, but is
also the form of being of the believer's own "inner
man." Not that "spirit" is to be considered as if it
were, like "flesh," mere substance. It is essentially
power, energy, and as such is "life-giving" ("quicken-
ing"). "Spirit" is therefore not properly a term of individual psychology. Every man, so far as he has attained to truly mature life, partakes both of flesh and
of spirit.

The principle of individuality is the "organism"

("body.") This does not mean to Paul the structure of bone, flesh, and blood to which we give the name of body. It is the pure organic form which subsists through all changes of material particles. The physical organ which I possess today is different in all or most of its material particles from that which I possessed eight years ago. In so far as it has an organic identity and continuity it is my body none the less. Thus for Paul the identity of the "organism" or "body" was in nowise affected by any change in its substance. The "flesh" might pass away, and "splendour" or light-substance be substituted, and the organism remain intact and self-identical. Thus Paul's insistence on the resurrection of the "body" is meant to assert the continuity of individual identity, as distinguished from the persistence of some impalpable shade or "soul" which was not in any real sense the identical man. Paul could not have talked of "saving souls"; it was the "emancipation of the body" that interested him, i.e. of the individual, self-identical, organic whole. The phrase in the Apostles' Creed, "the resurrection of the flesh," would have horrified him. He neither expected nor wished the "flesh" to rise again; he wished the "body" to be emancipated from the bonds of the "flesh." [5] It is probably on this analogy that we are meant to interpret the "emancipation of the creation." It, too, has somehow a "body" which can be redeemed from decay and clothed with splendour in the eternal world.[6]

The metaphysical distinction of two planes of being does not precisely correspond to ethical distinctions. It is often stated that Paul accepted a current view of his time, that spirit alone is good and matter essentially evil. He did not accept any such view. On the one hand there are "spiritual forces of wickedness";[7] and on the other hand what is wrong with the material world is not its moral evil, but its subjection to the futility of a perpetual flux of birth and decay.

That subjection is traced not, as in some contemporary theories, to the sin of Adam, for whose sake the earth was believed to have been "cursed," but vaguely to the will of God, i.e. it is in the nature of things as they are, though not of necessity permanent.[8]

In man, however, the case is complicated. By some means the "flesh" of mankind (which carries with it the *psyché*) has fallen under the dominion of sin, thus becoming not merely morally indifferent, though perishable matter, but "flesh of sin." This Sin is a mysterious power, not native to man or to the material world, but intruding into human nature on its lower side. Paul speaks of it in personal terms: it lives, reigns, holds us in slavery; it is condemned and overcome. Whether he was consciously personifying an abstraction, or whether Sin was for him really a personal power, like the Devil of popular mythology, is not clear. At all events it is not an inherent taint in matter, but rather one of the "spiritual forces of wickedness." [9]

How Sin came into human nature is a question which Paul does not answer very satisfactorily. He sometimes traces it to an historic transgression of a human ancestor in the remote past. This was the common account given in contemporary Judaism.[10] But in other passages he suggests a different origin. In the background of his world stand the "world-rulers" or "elemental spirits." They have some special relation to the material world, and it does not appear that in relation to it they are necessarily evil. But if man becomes subject to them, then he is fallen to a state of unnatural slavery. The process appears to be after this fashion: the reason of man, being a spark of the divine, knew God and read His law written on the heart; but instead of worshipping God and doing His will, it stooped to adore material forms, and thereby fell under the dominion of the elemental powers. The elevation of the material to the place of God led to the perversion of man's naturally right instincts. Reason itself became "reprobate" and the whole life of mankind was thrown into disorder.[11] If the transmitted sin of Adam is the characteristically Jewish doctrine, the theory of elemental spirits starts rather from Greek ideas. Neither can satisfy us, though each has hints of truth: on the one hand, the solidarity of humanity and the incalculable effects of individual transgression; on the other, the peril of exalting the physical and material to a dominance which is not in accord with man's real nature.

What might have been the relations of flesh and spirit had not sin intervened is a question on which Paul does not speculate. Taking things as they are, he scans history and sees that everywhere the power of evil has degraded man from the high estate he should hold, making even the "inner man," the reason which knew God, the conscience which witnessed to His law, slave to the material part and share in its fate of decay and futility. In the "flesh" sin has its seat. Reason may bow to the "flesh" and thereby fall under the dominion of sin and decay, but its nature remains alien from sin. "Flesh," on the other hand, has assimilated itself to the evil power, and the taint passes to the *psyché* or "soul" of which it is the organ, so that "the desires of the flesh and of the intellect" stand for the evil tendency in man. "The Flesh" therefore, in a moral sense, does not mean matter as evil in itself, but man's emotional and intellectual nature as perverted by sin and enslaved to material forces.[12]

It will be evident from this that "sin" is not for Paul identical with actual moral transgression of which the individual is fully conscious and for which he is fully responsible. That is the sense in which the word has been generally used by subsequent writers; but if it is taken in that sense, then Paul is inevitably misunderstood. The actual Greek word used (*hamartia*), like its equivalent in the Hebrew of the Old Testament, originally meant "missing the mark," or as we might say, "going wrong." Now whatever subtleties may complicate the discussion of such questions as moral responsibility and degrees of merit, at least it is plain that there is something wrong with mankind. There is a racial, a corporate, a social wrongness of which we are made in some sense partakers by the mere fact of our being born into human society. That is the meaning of "original sin," as the theologians call it. It is not the figment of an inherited guilt; how could anything so individual as guilty responsibility be inherited? It is a corporate wrongness in which we are involved by being men in this world. The purport of Paul's rather clumsy metaphysics is to show how the problem of evil in man is more than the problem of a series of sinful acts, which of his own free will he can stop if he makes up his mind to it. To some minds this distinction will seem artificial. They will agree with the child who refused to repeat the prayer "God make me a good girl," with the remark, "I wouldn't trouble God about a little thing like that: I can be good by myself if I want to." But a majority, perhaps, of those who take life seriously find that the trouble lies deeper. There is a deep-grained wrongness about human life as it is. The preoccupation with that wrongness as the primary interest of the religious life is certainly morbid; but no matter how freely and fully we recognize the wonderful potentialities of that human nature which we share, it remains true that there is a flaw somewhere, which defies simple treatment.

The monstrous development of the doctrine of "total depravity" and the reaction against it, have partly blinded us to the reality of what Paul called "sin in the flesh." That blindness has been partly connected with a fuller appreciation of individuality and individual responsibility than Paul had attained. But have we not placed an exaggerated emphasis upon individual responsibility? And is not that partly why

the whole idea of sin (in the sense in which evan-
gelical theology has used the term) has seemed to
be invalidated by the modern re-discovery of solidarity, and the recognition of the influence of heredity and social environment? It would indeed be difficult to say definitely of any particular wrong act that
its perpetrator was absolutely and exclusively responsible for it. When we have said that, it is often
thought that the whole Christian doctrine of sin is dis-
proved. It does not touch that doctrine as taught by
Paul. He thought of the "flesh," or lower nature of
man, as a *continuum* in which we all partake; and of
that "flesh" as having acquired by some means an impulse towards what is wrong. We should set aside his
terminology, and seek some other explanation of the
fact; but on the fact we must surely agree with Paul,
that there is something common, something racial
about sin in his sense of the term. It is a tendency
transmitted by heredity and deepened by environment, and its issues, like its sources, are not individual
merely, but racial. No one of us can disown his part
in the complicated evils in which society is entangled.
We are wrong, and we need to be put right. No casuistry explaining away the measure of individual responsibility makes much difference here: the fact of
wrongness remains. Our problem is Paul's problem.
Indeed, with the modern emphasis on solidarity, and
our rebelliousness against social evil in the world, the
problem is pressing on us with a peculiar urgency.
Perhaps, therefore, we may give ear afresh to a
teacher out of that ancient imperial world when he
sets before us his thoughts upon its solution. As we
shall see, he finds the point of attack upon this gigan-
tic force of wrong in the individual, though not in the
individual as an isolated unit.

For the moment, however, we are concerned to
pursue the trail of corporate wrong. For it brings disastrous consequences which also are corporate as well

as individual. Human history is a moral order, in
which it is impossible to be wrong without incurring
disaster. This disaster Paul calls, in traditional language, "The Wrath," or much more rarely, "The
Wrath of God." It has been supposed that Paul
thought of God as a vengeful despot, angry with men
whom nevertheless He had Himself created with the
liability to err, even if He did not create them to be
damned for His greater glory. That is a mere carica-
ture of Paul's view. There are, indeed, many indica-
tions in his use of language that "The Wrath of God"
is not being thought of as a passion of anger in the
mind of God. It is not without significance that there
are no more than three or possibly four passages
where the expression "The Wrath of God" (or "His
Wrath") appears at all, while the phrase "The Wrath"
is constantly used in a curiously impersonal way. Paul
carefully avoids ever making God the subject of the
verb "to be angry." Once he speaks of God as "apply-
ing the Wrath"—a strange way of saying that God
made His anger felt, if anger was thought of as a passion in the divine mind. It suggests rather a process
directed or controlled by a person.[13] Even in the passage which has about it most of the sterner colours of
Pharisaic theology the "vessels of Wrath" are the objects of God's forbearance; a statement which, if it
does not rule out the idea that God is angry with the
persons on whom at the same time He shows mercy,
at least gives a startling paradox if Paul is supposed
to have the thought of an angry God in mind.[14]

Let us, then, consider the one passage where "The
Wrath of God" is spoken of in more than an allusive
way. "The Wrath of God is being revealed," he says
to the Romans: it is to be seen at work in contemporary history. How, then? In earthquake, fire and brim-
stone? "God gave them up in the lusts of their own
hearts to impurity"; "God gave them up to disgraceful
passions"; "God gave them up to their reprobate rea-

son." "The Wrath of God," therefore, as seen in actual operation, consists in leaving sinful human nature to "stew in its own juice." [15] This is a sufficiently terrible conception, but if we believe, as Paul did, in any measure of human free will, what else is to happen if men choose steadfastly to ignore God? Are they not self-condemned to the reaping of the harvest of their sinful deeds, which is "a reprobate reason"—a disordered moral being, where the very instincts that should have led to good are perverted to the service of wrong? "If the light that is in thee be darkness, how great is that darkness!" And this "reprobation," be it observed, is the consequence of the rejection of that knowledge of God which is native to man. "The Wrath," then, is revealed before our eyes as the increasing horror of sin working out its hideous law of cause and effect. "The judgment" which overtakes sin is the growing perversion of the whole moral atmosphere of human society, which cannot but affect to a greater or less degree every individual born into it. Meanwhile, the characteristic personal activity of God is not wrath but "kindness," "long-suffering," rooted in His love and ready to display itself in "grace." [16] That is why "The Wrath" is not the last word of the moral order for Paul. The "wages of sin" is real and terrible; it is moral decay and death for the race. But that is not a complete account of the moral universe. "God justifies the ungodly." [17] To this matter we shall presently turn. The intention of this chapter is to set forth the problem of sin as Paul faced it, and to suggest how close to reality he was when he placed his finger on the point that sin is a racial and social fact, in which every individual is implicated, and that if the moral order is nothing more than a law of retribution, there is nothing before sinful man but greater sin and moral disaster.[18]

The whole of this is only preparatory to a decisive declaration of the way out of apparently desperate conditions. Even so, does it give too gloomy a view? We like to think that humanity left to itself would grow better. But would it? Is it not true that whole nations and societies of men have sunk lower and lower out of sheer inner rottenness, often bringing other peoples down with them in their fall, since there is a solidarity of mankind? And is such a future for our species as the ghastly imaginings of Mr. Wells's "Time Machine" wholly inconceivable? But Jesus Christ, we are told, whom Paul professed to follow, took no such gloomy view of human nature and its prospects. It may be granted at once that there is a difference of emphasis between the Master and His disciple. There was a good reason for this. Jesus worked among the Jews, where the dominant theology took a gloomy enough view of the nature of all men except a very few. It was therefore His first and chief care to give hope to those who seemed hopeless and to assure them of the glorious possibilities open to them in the love of the Father in heaven. Paul worked among the pagans, where real downright evil was readily condoned and glozed over, and its inevitable consequences explained away, while none the less the rottenness of sin was eating into the heart of that corrupt civilization, despite all the efforts of moralists and legislators. "The Wrath" that follows sin was actually being revealed; and it was part of Paul's task to open the eyes of the pagan world to it, that they might be willing to seek the better way. But we cannot quote Jesus against Paul as giving an easy and cheerfully optimistic view of the actual state of human society. On the contrary, there is enough in His teaching to show that He too saw the society of His day "rushing down a steep place into the sea," with no hope of its redemption save in the "Sovereignty of God." [19] Therein Paul was His true interpreter to the wider world.

VI

THE TYRANNY OF AN IDEA

We have now to approach that region of our subject where Paul's contribution is perhaps most original and characteristic, and where at the same time it is most cumbered with temporary elements: his treatment of the idea of Law. The enormous importance which attached to that idea in contemporary Judaism, and particularly in the Pharisaic branch of it to which Paul belonged, has already been indicated. Paul's attitude to the historic Law of Moses is curiously contradictory on the surface. On the one hand it reflects for him that inexorable moral order which is in the nature of things. The nature of things is the will of God, and the law which reflects it must be of God, and therefore holy, spiritual, just and good.[1] On the other hand he detests this law as the supreme instrument of slavery (why, we shall see presently). It is not unfair to regard this deep paradox in his thought as the penalty of a false upbringing, which had implanted almost a morbid *idée fixe* that he never threw off. His training and prepossessions made it for ever impossible for him to take a detached view of the Law in which he had been taught to see the eternal will of

God. He might reasonably have attacked its mixing
upon equal terms of ritual trivialities and awful moral
principles. He did not do so. His training made it impossible. The Law was a vast and indivisible system
which must somehow be accounted for as a whole.
His entire mental background made things peculiarly
hard for him at this point. But it was not without advantage that Christian thought was thus led to face
with the utmost definition the conflict which under-
lay the attack that Jesus Christ had made upon the
organized religion of His day.

The attitude of Jesus to the Jewish Law was singularly free and unembarrassed. He made full use of it
as an impressive statement of high ethical ideals.
Even its ritual practices He treated with perfect tolerance where they did not conflict with fundamental
moral obligations. From Pharisaic formalism He appealed to the relative simplicity of the venerable written law. But again from the written law itself He appealed to the basic rights and duties of humanity: the
Sabbath was made for man, not man for the Sabbath;
the Law might permit the dissolution of marriage, but
there was something more deeply rooted in the nature
of things which forbade it; the *lex talionis,* the central principle of legal justice, must go overboard in the
interests of the holy impulse to love your neighbour
not merely as yourself, but as God has loved you.
Such free-handed dealing meant that the whole notion of morality as a code of rules with sanctions of re-
ward and punishment was abandoned. But the aver-
age Christian was slow to see this implication. For
instance, Jesus had taken fasting out of the class of
meritorious acts, and given it a place only as the fit-
ting and spontaneous expression of certain spiritual
states. This is what an early authoritative catechism of
the Church made of His teaching: "Let not your
fasts be with the hypocrites, for they fast on Monday

and Thursday; ye therefore shall fast on Wednesday and Friday." [2] It sounds ludicrous, but we may ask, Was it not on some very similar principle that the Church did actually carry through its reconstruction of "religious observance"? And a Church which so perverted Christ's treatment of the ritual law proved itself almost equally incapable of understanding His drastic revision of the moral law.

It was therefore of the utmost importance that one who knew from the inside the system which Jesus attacked should, through being compelled to confront his own exaggerated legalism with His Master's independence, point the way to the more fundamental implications of what Jesus had done. Paul found himself driven to reconsider, not this precept or that, but the whole nature of law as such; and it is a mark of his real greatness that he did so on the basis, not of theory merely, but of experience. In its elements, moreover, the experience on which he founded was wider than that of a Pharisaic Jew. For it is not of any peculiarly Jewish experience that he speaks. For himself, no doubt, whether as Jew or as Christian, the so-called Law of Moses was absolute law. Within the sphere of law there was nothing higher or more perfect. Yet the identical principle appeared also among the pagans. The pagan sense of right and wrong was God's law written on the heart—the same law as that delivered on Sinai, Paul would have said, though more doubtfully, obscurely, and imperfectly revealed. He had sympathy enough to perceive that the Stoic too must fall upon this problem of a law which he could not but acknowledge as divine, which yet condemned him without giving him strength to do better. There are passages in Stoic writers tinged with a melancholy which recalls the moving transcript from Paul's experience in the seventh chapter of his Epistle to the Romans. It is at bottom a human problem, and not a specifically Jewish one, that he is facing, but his own bitter experience in Pharisaic Judaism lent a cutting edge to his analysis.

The education of the youthful Paul in his Jewish home at Tarsus must have been a very rigorous one. We may compare it with the strictest kind of Puritan training which in England, and still more perhaps in Scotland and Wales, moulded the lives of a former generation. He was early drilled into a very high standard of personal purity and probity. As he grew up he found that his food and clothes, the way he washed his hands, the way he had his hair cut, and all the simplest operations of a boy's daily life were rigidly prescribed,[3] and were so distinct from those of other Tarsian boys that he was bound to ask, Why? He was told, Because the God of our fathers has commanded it in His law, as He has also commanded us not to kill or steal; and if we do otherwise, the wrath of God will come upon us. So he came to think of this God as very strong and holy, but also very stern and jealous. He was a merciful God too, but His mercy was chiefly shown in the inestimable gift of the Law to Israel, His darling people.[4] Through that gift they knew, and only they, the eternal rule of life by which alone happiness could be attained. "See, I set before you this day a blessing and a curse": so the young Paul learned to recite out of Deuteronomy. To know the Law and keep it in its entirety was the assured way to perfect blessedness. To infringe the least of its precepts was to bring down the vengeance of a justly incensed God, "an eye for an eye, and a tooth for a tooth." Such was the eternal justice, which God must vindicate, because He was God.[5] And the Law itself in all its precepts was a pattern for human life framed upon this eternal justice, with its root principle of reciprocity or retribution. This Law had been given, in the inscrutable providence of God, to His chosen people as the supreme mark of His favour.

So Paul was taught at home; and as he looked upon the Greek boys he passed in the street, he was proud to think that he had a secret denied to them all—he knew the Law. Its possession undoubtedly brought to an earnest-minded Jew a real moral elevation. Such writings as the hundred and nineteenth Psalm show with what enthusiasm a pious Jew could contemplate this great gift of God to his race. "Oh, how I love Thy law! It is my meditation all the day." We may think of Paul as sharing in such emotions in his study of the Law, especially from the time when, aiming at the Rabbinate, he devoted himself wholly to it. Out of this concentration upon the Law grew on the one side an intense national pride, on the other an overwhelming sense of the moral order with its awful principle of retribution. Both were affronted by the discovery in Palestine, when he went there, of those renegade Jews the Nazarenes, whose leader had set himself up against the Law and denounced its authorized interpreters, and had at last been cast out of the commonwealth of Israel for blasphemy against God's Temple and His Holy Name. It was a grim enthusiasm for the moral order which made Paul a persecutor, as it has made many another. "Saul, Saul, why persecutest thou Me?" Paul might have thought he had his answer ready: "Because the moral order must be vindicated and the law-breaker punished." Yet when the question was actually pressed home he found he had no answer.

For while outwardly Paul was the proud, irreproachable champion of the Law, inward struggles plunged his soul in darkness and confusion. The weakness of his human nature had revealed itself in conflict with the absolute claims of the moral law. The sense of impotence and despair that took hold upon him is reflected in one of the most moving passages of his writings, the seventh chapter of the Epistle to the Romans. It is not without significance that the example he there uses to illustrate his point is the one commandment in the Decalogue which is concerned with thought and not with overt word or act. "Thou shalt not covet," said the Law. We may recall that covetousness is noted in the Gospels as a special snare of the pious Pharisee. From his Pharisaic days Paul was well aware that morality must cover the inner life of feeling, thought, motive, and desire. "He is not a Jew who is such only outwardly" [6] is a sentence he might have written at any time in his life. Now, it appears, he found that even though he might conform his outward actions to the requirements of the Law he could not control his thoughts and desires. But the Law was a single whole; to break one precept was to renounce all.[7] He was as honest and strict with himself as he was severe with others, and he fell under the scourge of self-condemnation. He loved the Law, consented to it as good, rejoiced in it "after the inner man," as he says, but he could not keep it. "The good I would, I do not, and the evil I would not, that I do . . . when I would do good, evil is present with me."

It is at this point that Paul's experience as a Pharisee falls in with the common experience of men. It was not a Jew who wrote *"Video meliora proboque, deteriora sequor."* The moral incompetence of human nature in the presence of an acknowledged ideal is no private discovery. A man may perceive the ideal clearly, and contemplate it with a keen æsthetic delight, and yet desires and impulses which contradict it may be so much more real to him that his actual conduct is a perpetual denial of the ideal. This divided state of the personality is a state of miserable impotence, in which the freedom of the will is a mere illusion. "The freedom of the will," writes a modern psychologist,[8] "may be a doctrine which holds true of the healthy, and indeed the exercise of will and determination is the normal way in which to summon the resources of power; but the doctrine that the will alone is the way to power is a most woebegone theory for the relief of the morally sick—and who of us is whole? Freedom to choose? Yes! But what if, when we choose, we have no power to perform? We open the sluice-gates, but the channels are dry; we pull the lever, but nothing happens; we try by our will to summon up our strength, but no strength comes." No wonder Paul described such a condition as a state of slavery.

Most of us know something about this condition, though few of us are reduced to the depths of despair to which Paul came. We pacify a not very exacting conscience with a rough approximation. But the question may be raised, whether this half-conscious tolerance of a real though unacknowledged rift between ideal and practice is not a form of "suppressed complex" which works more injury than we commonly imagine. Worse certainly is the state of the person who is sentimental enough to think that to admire what is noble is a sufficient substitute for doing it. Worst of all is the actual hypocrisy of pretending to ourselves that by great rigour in practices we find easy we can tip the balance even, and

> *Compound for sins that we're inclined to*
> *By damning those we have no mind to.*

Such hypocrisy is often a form of instinctive self-protection, and it is most common where moral ideals have been reduced to the most precise and comprehensive rules of life. That is probably why the Puritan of literature is so often a hypocrite, and likewise the Pharisee of the Gospels, whose religion was discipline pressed to an even more logical extreme. Paul was not that kind of Pharisee. He was earnest, clear-sighted, and absolutely honest with himself. He could find no way out of the *impasse*. He could not keep the Law, especially in its most inward and spiritual

precepts, which sought to rule the thoughts and
motives. But law must be upheld. It was in the nature of things, and God must needs vindicate it.
Where then was any door of hope for Paul the sinner?

We now come to the turning-point in Paul's career.
He set out for Damascus, the fierce avenger of an
outraged Law; but in his heart he felt that the Law
had broken him, and hope was almost gone. "Who
will rescue me from the clutch of this dead body?" is
his bitter cry. . . . Time passes, and we meet a new
Paul. The terror of the Law has passed from his soul,
with all the miserable sense of moral impotence:
"There is now no condemnation"; "I can do anything in Him who gives me strength." And he has
now no further thought of inflicting the terrors of the
Law upon others. He who once "breathed out threat-
enings and slaughter" is now content if he may bear
his share of the sufferings by which others may be
saved: "I am glad of my sufferings for you; I am making up in my own flesh the deficit of Christ's sufferings for His Body, which is the Community"; "I am
crucified with Christ." [9] What we observe in all this
is that the preoccupation with law, and more precisely with its principle of retribution, has slipped
away; and in the freedom and peace of mind that
ensues Paul has gained the "heart at leisure from
itself" and open to all tides of human sympathy. He
has discovered some new secret of life. What is it?

"God who said 'Light shall flash out of darkness'
flashed upon our hearts and enlightened us with a
knowledge of the splendour of God in the face of
Christ." [10] It was a new perception of God that had
come to Paul. The God of Pharisaism was like the
God of the Deists. He stood aloof from the world
He had made, and let law take its course. He did not
here and now deal with individual sinful men. Paul
lets us see how new and wonderful was the experience, when God "flashed on his heart" in personal

dealing with him. He had not suspected that God was like that. His theological studies had told him that God was loving and merciful; but he had thought this love and mercy were expressed once and for all in the arrangements he had made for Israel's blessedness— "the plan of salvation." It was a new thing to be assured by an inward experience admitting of no further question that God loved him, and that the eternal mercy was a Father's free forgiveness of His erring child. This was the experience that Christ had brought him: he had seen the splendour of God's own love in the face of "the Son of God, who loved me and gave Himself for me." [11] What knowledge of Jesus Christ and His teaching lay behind the flash of enlightenment it is now impossible for us to say; but it is clear that the God whom Paul met was the "Father" of Jesus' own Gospel parables, the "Shepherd" who goes after the one sheep until He finds it. It was the God, in fact, whom the whole of the life of Jesus set forth, to the astonishment of those among whom He moved. Living still, He brought God to men in the same unmistakable way. The divine love that through Jesus had found Zacchæus the publican had now through the risen Jesus found Paul the Pharisee. Henceforward the central facts of life for Paul were that while he was yet a sinner God had found and forgiven him, and that this was the work of Jesus Christ in whose love the love of God had become plain. About those two *foci* in experience his theology revolves.[12]

In order to establish against those who impugned it the validity of his new experience of God, Paul set out to discover in what were to him and to his critics indisputable facts, the proof of his assertion. The interest of these discussions for us is limited to the extent to which they illuminate on various sides the new conception of God and His dealings which had come to Paul in experience. His argument comes to this, that while the Law had a place of its own in the providential order, it never did and never could exhaust the whole truth about God and man. Law worked wholly within the sphere of reciprocity or recompense. But history showed that such reciprocity was at least very irregular and incomplete in its operation. In the first place, his critics must grant that in God's dealings with the ancestors of the "Chosen people" there was an element of free choice on God's part, altogether out of relation to the deserts of the objects of that choice. Abraham was called even before he had taken upon him the rite of circumcision. Jacob was loved by God, as the Scripture showed, before he had done either good or ill. That indicated a freedom of choice on God's part which was incompatible with the strict working of law.[13] Such freedom of choice, however, raises a new difficulty—the case of the "rejects." They are left in sin, and must on the principles of law pay the inexorable penalty of sin in ever greater and greater sin until complete moral disaster and death is the result. But what actually happens? "What if God, with all His will to exhibit His wrath and make known His power, bore very patiently with 'vessels of wrath,' fit only for destruction?" [14] There is a flaw, that is, in the working of the system of recompense. "In this, O Lord," exclaims a contemporary Pharisaic writer, "shall Thy righteousness and goodness be declared, if Thou wilt compassionate them that have no wealth of good works." [15] The writer of these words is clearly very uncertain whether God's compassion does actually reach so far. Paul, like most Pharisees, is sure that in all ages a remnant at least has found unmerited mercy of God, even though His normal principle was retribution. In other words, forgiveness is, and always has been, a fact verifiable in the experience of some men at least. But it is wholly inconsistent with the law of retribution. "Do you make light," Paul wrote, "of

the wealth of His kindness and tolerance and patience? Do you not know that the kindness of God is
trying to lead you to repentance?" [16] In practice, that
is to say, the Law as an absolute system of recompense has wrecked itself upon the character of God
as loving and pitiful. But this very fact that God has
passed over, or "winked at," sin in spite of the Law,
indicates the logical necessity for some different principle to be disclosed.[17]

Next, and arguing still from facts which would be
admitted by his Pharisaic opponents to facts which
they were attempting to deny, Paul showed that
within the Jewish system itself a principle different
from the legal principle was to be found. This seems
so obvious to us, to whom the prophetic element is
the heart of the Old Testament, as hardly to need
labouring. But to the Pharisees the Law was the
foundation of all, the prophets merely commentary.
In effect, Paul challenged them to interpret the Law
by the prophets, and to find, even in the books of the
Law itself, statements suggesting a personal relation
to God over and above the merely legal relation to
Him as governor of the universe. In effect he says to
his critics, "*You* cannot find a place for these sayings:
I can." And so he shows that the Christian revelation
of God is the fulfilment of a logical necessity in the
heart of the old religion.[18]

But further, the system of legal retribution was
fitted, Paul argued, to exhibit God's wrath, but *not,* in
the full sense, His righteousness. That is a startling
statement addressed to any Jewish public of the first
century—or for that matter to the bulk of "Christian"
opinion today. Yet it was a thought not unfamiliar
to the prophets, that God's righteousness is shown in
making His people righteous.[19] God must show Himself, says Paul, at once "just and justifier." [20] For all the
scholastic language, there is here a very vital truth:
that righteousness, or justice, is a bigger thing than

mere reciprocity.[21] It is the point which Jesus Christ made when He drily observed that a man's field gets sun and rain whether he has deserved these good things or not, and when He likened God to an employer so lost to all sense of justice as to pay a day's wage for an hour's work.[22] God must, by an inner necessity of His nature, do good to men: His "property is to have mercy and to forgive." But within the sphere of law there is no place for forgiveness. If righteousness or justice is retribution, as law assumes, then forgiveness is unrighteous. Once more there is a logical necessity for the revelation of something other than law.

The real dilemma, therefore, which Paul places before his opponents is this: If you are once agreed that the ethical is the basis of all relation of God to man, then you are bound to deal with the moral law of retribution. It appears to be the very foundation of morality, and yet it conflicts with the religious instinct which says, "God is not like that." Until you can clear scores with the principle of retribution, you will be haunted by it in all your attempts to give play to the grace of God. As we have seen, some of Paul's Jewish compatriots, even of his fellow-Pharisees, found themselves able in some measure to hold to the legal principle and yet to find a "little door" for the grace of God. But if you are taking morality seriously, this position cannot be stable, and indeed Christianity itself, failing to understand or follow Paul, has given proof how if you persist in identifying righteousness with retributive justice, and then insist that God must be righteous or just before He is merciful, you cannot let the character of God have that effective power in the religious and moral life which belongs to it.

Yet law serves a purpose. After all, the moral order of retribution which it embodies is a real fact, though it is not the only relevant fact, nor the final and decisive fact. If Paul had worked with the idea of development or "evolution," he might have explained the place of law as a necessary stage in that development. Indeed he comes very near to doing so. "The Law," he says, "was our 'pedagogue,' until Christ should come." Those words have been interpreted as though they described the Law as a preparatory education, continued at a higher stage by Christ. That, however, is not quite what Paul meant. The "pedagogue" in Greek society was not a "schoolmaster." He did not give lessons (at least that was not his natural function). He was a slave who accompanied a boy to school, and both waited upon him and also exercised a supervision which interfered with the boy's freedom of action. He is, in fact, a figure in the little allegory which Paul gives us to illustrate the position of the People of God before Christ came. There was a boy left heir to a great estate. He was a minor, and so must have guardians and trustees. He was as helpless in their hands as if he had been a slave. He must live on the allowance they gave him, and follow their wishes from day to day. They gave him a "pedagogue" to keep him out of mischief. He could not please himself, or realize his own purposes and ambitions. Yet all the time he was the heir; the estate was his and no one else's. Just so the People of God, the Divine Commonwealth, was cramped and fettered by ignorance and evil times. It remained in uneasy expectation of one day coming into active existence. At last the heir came of age: guardians and trustees abdicated their powers, and the grown man possessed in full realization all that was his. So now the fettered life of the Divine Commonwealth bursts its bonds and comes into active existence.

The law therefore appears as a necessary but transitory stage of discipline. It was not fundamental to God's dealings with His sons. In the same passage

Paul points out, in his scholastic fashion, that historically the Law came four hundred years after the
"promise" had been given to "faithful Abraham"; and
the "testament" by which God devised His blessing
upon Abraham could not be reversed by a codicil
added four hundred years later! [23] In other words,
the intervention of law was not a reversal of God's
original and eternal purpose of pure love and grace
towards men: it only subserved that purpose, while
it seemed to contradict it, just as the presence of the
"pedagogue" might seem to the high-spirited young
heir quite contrary to the rights secured to him by
his father's will.

How then did the Law subserve the purpose realized in Christ? Paul's answer is so startling that his
commentators have been reluctant to take his words
in their plain meaning. "The Law," he says, "came in,
by a side wind, in order that there might be more
transgression"! [24] If Paul often talked like that, we can
understand how he shocked the good folk at Jerusalem, Jews and Christians alike! Yet there is no great
difficulty in resolving the paradox. The Law came in,
not to increase "sin," of course, but to increase *transgression*. We have seen that for Paul "sin" is a state
of the Race, in which things have gone wrong, quite
apart from any consideration of a conscious or deliberate wrongdoing on the part of any individual. "Before law came, sin was in the world, but sin is not
imputed where there is no law." [25] The knowledge of
the moral law confronts the sinful state with a rule of
goodness, and by the contrast brings home the wrong
to the conscience as guilt.

An examination of the seventh chapter of Romans
makes this clear. We have already treated that
chapter as an index to Paul's state of mind just before
his conversion. But the passage is ideal biography
rather than a strict transcript "from the life." It starts
with the description of an "age of innocence," which

for the individual as for the race is an inference of
reason or a figment of the imagination rather than
strict history. There never was a time when Paul, or
when the human race, was self-conscious without also
being in some rudimentary way conscious of moral
obligation. Yet by comparison with later stages we
may use as a working concept the notion of an "age
of innocence." By that is meant, not that one did no
wrong, but that one had no sense of any contrast between what one actually did and what one ought to
have done. "Once I lived my own life, without any
law," Paul puts it. But while that stage remained
there was no chance of better things. The establish-
ment of a clear distinction between right and wrong
was essential. Yet it is probably true that in every
normal case this distinction emerged in conscience
as the sense of having done wrong, the sense of guilt
or shame, essentially humiliating and painful. "Law
came to life—and I died." Then follows the phase of
struggle and defeat, with which we have already
dealt.

It is necessary here to distinguish between two
counts which Paul brings against law. He found that
the knowledge that a thing was wrong provoked him
to seek it, so that to that degree law actually in-
creased "sin." The fact is sufficiently attested in
proverbial lore—"stolen fruits are pleasant!"—to stand
as a widespread experience. But it is not so important
or perhaps so universal as Paul seems to have thought;
or at least it is scarcely so important universally as it
appears to have been for him. In any case it rather
obscures his main point, which is this: Every individual of the human race is so entangled in the general
"wrongness" that he has no power, left to himself, to
avoid committing constantly acts which, whether he
knows it or not, add to the sum of the wrong. To know
that these acts are wrong does not prevent him from
doing them, for "the law is weak through the flesh";[26]

but it does imprint upon his conscience in the indelible characters of shame and guilt the contrast of good and evil. It brings "sin" home, from being a general state of the human race, to be a conscious burden upon the mind of the individual. It is no longer "sin" merely; it is "transgression."

We may compare the condition which Aristotle describes as "incontinence,"[27] the essence of which is that the individual now knows, as he did not at a lower stage, that the things he is doing are wrong, and yet cannot keep himself from them. Aristotle makes this state the natural approach to the next higher, that of "continence," in which the things known to be wrong are through struggle and effort gradually discarded. Similarly, Paul sees that it is a great advance to have discovered sin in one's own heart as guilt. Only the man who is conscious of his guilt can be saved from the sin of which he is guilty. Only as the individual acknowledges such guilt can the racial wrongness be successfully attacked. In this sense, the function of law as "increasing guilt" can be regarded as part of a beneficent divine plan. But only if there is something else to follow. Otherwise we may give up all hope. Paul's charge against the Judaism in which he was brought up was that its view of the world went no further than the merely legal stage. Perhaps his statement of the case was sometimes too sweeping. Surely he would have admitted that at all times it was *possible* even within Judaism for men to transcend the purely legal attitude, and that as a matter of fact many saints of the old order had done so. This is, indeed, implied in his references to Elijah's Seven Thousand and Isaiah's Remnant. But in the main the highest moralists of his time did actually see no further than a system which attempted to build the moral life of man exclusively upon that principle of reciprocity which they discerned in the nature of things, and allowed no real place for a fresh, direct, personal act of the loving, gracious God whom yet they professed to worship. Paul held that this God had indeed framed a universe in which the principle of retribution was at work: for he never denied that the Law largely answered to real facts, and certainly he never doubted that evil is ultimately disastrous and good ultimately blessed. The conception of a right which should be defeated at the end of the day did not dawn upon his mind: that was left for Mr. Bertrand Russell. But this whole universe, with all its complex reactions, he held to have been constituted by God to the end that through it man might rise to a higher order, that of the "sons of God." At that point the "pedagogue" must step aside, and God's heir claim his freedom.

VII

THE SON OF GOD

"What the law could not do, because it was powerless through our lower nature, that God did, by sending His own Son."[1] From what has already been said it should be clear that the problem before Paul was not "How can a just God forgive sin?" but "Granted that God is by His nature both 'just and justifier,' i.e. that because He is righteous He must forgive sin and impact righteousness, how is that righteousness to be made available for man?" It is therefore not a problem of the adjustment of abstract principles of justice and mercy, but of the relations of God and man on the personal plane. Man must discover himself as a son of God. With this in view, "When the full time had arrived, God sent out His Son, born of a woman, born in subjection to law, in order that He might emancipate those who were subject to law, i.e. that we might receive adoption into sonship."[2]

It is not here proposed to attempt any discussion in detail of what is called the "Christology" of Paul. It is a highly speculative structure of thought, making use of a difficult philosophical vocabulary. As a philosophy it is compounded of various elements, not easily disentangled. First, already in pre-Christian times there was a highly elaborated body of Jewish doctrine concerning the Messiah. Implying at one time no more than an ideal Hebrew prince of the dynasty of David, the conception had attracted to itself some of the most mystical elements in Jewish religious thought. At the beginning of the Christian era the Messiah was widely thought of as an eternal Being, called "The Son of Man," or "The Man," as though He were the type or representative of humanity, abiding with God from all eternity, partly revealed in vision and mystical experience to saints of all ages, such as Enoch and Ezra, but destined "in the fulness of time" to be openly manifested for the consummation of human history.[3] It may now be taken as certain that Jesus believed Himself to be Messiah, and shaped His life and went to His death in conviction. The only question is to what extent He shared various forms of contemporary belief about the Messiah, and in what ways He re-shaped the idea. It seems at least highly probable that He was the first to link the thought of the Messiah with that of the ideal "Servant of Jehovah" in the prophecies of the "Second Isaiah"—the Servant who would suffer and die that others might know God. Without further discussion, it will be plain that Paul was from the outset within the sphere of Messianic ideas, both in their traditional form in Pharisaic Judaism, and in the form in which from the life and teaching of Jesus they had passed into early Christian circles.

Further, Messianic beliefs had already, to some degree, become fused in certain types of Jewish thought with the idea of the "Wisdom" of God, by which He made the world, and by which He reveals Himself to man. And this in turn had been brought in contact with the Greek doctrine of the "Logos" or eternal Reason—the rational order of the universe, and the divine spark in man. Although Paul never actually identifies Christ with the "Logos," as the author of the Fourth Gospel does, yet in his attempt to understand the position of Christ in relation to man and his world he owes much to Logos speculation; and he does call Christ "The Wisdom of God," in so many words.[4]

In the world outside Judaism, the most living religions of the time generally centered in faith in a "Saviour-God," who was often believed to have lived, died, and risen again, and with whom the believer could win fellowship through certain rites. These were the so-called "mystery-religions." Their origins were various, their rites were sometimes wild and licentious, and in most the superstitions of magic and astrology played a part; but at best their offer of fellowship with a Saviour-God ministered to a real religious need of the time. The view has been put forward that Paul reacted from Judaism practically to a mystery-religion of the ordinary type, with Jesus Christ as its mythical Saviour-God. One need not be committed to any such paradoxical opinion, if one holds that he was influenced both in thought and language by these cults—probably not from personal knowledge, but because that sort of thing was "in the air" of the religious world at the time. His audience in the pagan world had not the background of Judaism. It did not know what he was talking about when he spoke of "the Christ" ("Messiah"); but when he spoke of "the Lord, the Saviour," the phrase at least conveyed some idea to their minds. Their highest religious experience had hitherto been associated with language of that kind, and it expressed an idea which could be filled in from the abundant material supplied by Christian experience and by the life and teaching of Jesus Himself. The Christian missionary in India, say, today, follows a not very different plan.

From such sources are the terms of Paul's "Christology" derived. But it cannot be too emphatically re-

peated that the thing he is talking about in these
terms is not a speculative idea, but a piece of real experience. That he had met Christ face to face he
never doubted; it was a part of his actual history. "It
pleased God to reveal His Son in me"; "last of all,
He was seen of me also"; "henceforth I am alive, and
yet not I, but Christ is alive in me; and the life which
I now live under physical conditions I live by virtue
of my trust in the Son of God, who loved me and gave
Himself for me." [5] This is the authentic language of
personal experience. Mr. H. G. Wells has told us that
what he means by "God" has a close resemblance to
what Paul meant by "Christ." [6] He is so far right that
each of these men is telling us of a personal meeting
with an unseen Friend and Leader, who is known at
once, intuitively, to be the Leader of humanity, and
the Friend of all who have yielded themselves to the
divine call sounding in the heart of man. So far as
one can judge, the chief specific differences in the experience of the two men are that Paul's "Christ" bears
the definite ethical lineaments of the historic Jesus,
and that, unlike Mr. Wells's "Invisible King," He has
a real and intimate relation to the whole universe and
its Creator. He is, in fact, the "Son of God"—the eternal type of all the relationship between personal beings and the personal Centre of reality. What Paul
saw in the vision that changed his life was "the splendour of God in the face of Christ." The Christ he met
is the "Wisdom of God" by which the worlds were
framed; that is, as we might put it, the ultimate meaning of all reality is no other than the meaning of the
life and character of Christ. But, like the "Invisible
King," Paul's Christ has had a history entwined with
the history of man. Man was made "in the image of
God": that "image" of God is Christ.[7] There is in men
a life derived from their natural progenitor, whom
Paul calls by the Hebrew word for man, "Adam."
But there is in men also a higher life, by which they

are linked with God and the eternal order. "The first man Adam became a living *psyché,* the last Adam, a life-giving Spirit. . . . The first man is earthy, of clay; the second Man is from Heaven." This second Adam or heavenly Man-in-men is Christ.[8] The people of God in their ancient pilgrimage "drank of the spiritual rock that followed them, and that rock is Christ";[9] or, as we might put it, the perpetual springs of the spiritual life of the Race are found in Him.

If we now recall what was said above of the dealings of God in history for the founding of the Divine Commonwealth, we shall see that in Paul's view every step in that direction was in some sense an act of Christ within humanity. And every such step led forward to some decisive act in which what was before obscure and halting should become definite and effective. Then at last "in the fulness of time," Christ came. By a gracious act of God, His Son was "sent forth"; or, to put the same thing in another way, by His own act of will, in absolute unity with the purpose of His Father, "He made Himself of no consequence, accepted the standing of a slave, and was born in human form; and so, presenting the appearance of a man, He stooped to a subordinate position, and persevered in it till death—a death on the gallows!" In other words, He who is always and everywhere the Man-in-men became *a man,* a Jew, a crucified criminal.[10]

So stated, the thought is by admission a difficult one. But there are certain points which need to be observed. The question in Paul's mind is not a question of the scarcely thinkable combination in one person of the contradictory attributes of transcendent Deity on the one hand and of a purely "natural" and non-divine humanity on the other. Humanity itself *means* Christ, and has no proper meaning without Him. Unless a man is a "son of God," he is so far less than man: he has yet to grow "to a mature man, i.e.

to the measure of the full stature of Christ." [11] The history of man is the story of the course by which mankind is becoming fully human. The controlling Mind in this history—the "life-giving Spirit" of the whole process—Paul conceives as a real personality, standing already in that relation to God in which alone man is fully human; already, and eternally, Son of God.

The emphasis, implied in Paul's teaching, upon the absolute importance of the entry of this Son of God into human history as an individual may be regarded as a part of the general movement of thought by which during these centuries the individual was for the first time being discovered, simultaneously with the transition from national or tribal to universal conceptions of human history. In the center of this movement stands the personality of Jesus Christ, intensely individual, and yet wonderfully universal—an individual who consciously gathered up in His hands the threads of history, and who has proved Himself through following ages to have a direct affinity with the most diverse types of man in all peoples. We can yet discern in Him a continuity with the universal higher impulses of humanity, and a personal command of men who are brought in touch with Him; and these are essentially the facts lying at the base of Paul's conception of the Son of God who became a man "in the fulness of time." To this, however, we have to add, what we shall presently consider, the definite achievement which Paul saw to have issued from the life and death of Jesus, and which stands as a solid part of history. It is on the ground of what He achieved historically that Paul identified Jesus with the Son of God who is the "life-giving Spirit" of humanity. This, it may be suggested, is a firmer ground for the building of a "Christology" than minute psychological analysis of the meager data concerning the self-consciousness of Jesus in the Gospels. Not that psychology is of no importance here; for the investigation of phenomena

of personality which seem to lie beyond the threshold
of ordinary individual consciousness may well lead us
nearer to an understanding of the greatest difficulty
in which Paul's teaching about Christ after all leaves
us—the union of the universal and the individual in
one personality.

In any case we must set it down as a very suggestive
element in Paul's thought, that he regards the whole
of the individual life of Jesus as a working-out of one
supra-historic act of self-sacrifice, in which we may see
the gathering-up of the whole impulse of self-sacrifice
to be found in the history of mankind. It is the
"life-giving Spirit" from whom all this comes, and
there was one human life which was entirely an expression of it, in that intense, purposive and deliberate
form which is proper only to individuality.[12] According
to Paul, not only had that life of self-sacrifice decisive
results for all men, but it marked a crisis also in the
life-history of Christ. By that humiliation He actually
attained a new relation to humanity and to God, for
"God highly exalted Him" to be Lord of the Race.[13]
Henceforward having by His earthly ministry and
death pioneered a highway for Himself into the hearts
of men, He dwells spiritually in conscious communion
with all those who are conformed to the image of His
dying, so that their life is hidden with Christ in God,
and on earth they form His body, "until He come." [14]
For a day is yet to come when Christ will be "revealed" in a new and fuller way, and with Him all
who share His life. And in a figurative or mythological
form Paul shows us Christ as the Captain of His redeemed, smiting His foes to the ground: and the last
of them is death. Then, Lord of a redeemed and
deathless universe, He makes the last sacrifice. As in
the hour of His humiliation He rendered up His body
and soul to God for the redemption of the world, so
now, its victorious King, He yields up the Body His
Spirit has created "that God may be all and in all." [15]

Such is in rough outline Paul's conception of the "historic Christ"—a Christ who has a history of His own, intimately connected at every stage with the history of Man from start to finish; and who appears as an individual to share man's life at a point historically determined by His own working as hidden Spirit in humanity. That appearance on earth as an individual is the crisis in the history both of Christ Himself and of the humanity He saves and leads. The ministry of Jesus, therefore, culminating in His death, is essential to Paul's whole thought. If in certain aspects of his theology it is the death that bulks most largely—because it seemed to him to be the purest and most moving expression of what the whole life meant—he is quite aware that the ethical impulse given by the example and teaching of Jesus is of the very stuff of the Christian life. He alludes to the Gospel story but sparingly, but those who study his teaching most closely become aware that he is himself acting and speaking all through under the impulse of the life and teaching of Jesus. If he refuses to "know Christ after the flesh," [16] it means that he will not risk a harking-back to the temporary conditions of the Galilæan ministry when the Spirit of Christ is clearly leading out into new fields. The issues of that ministry have been gathered up in the new experience of "Christ in me," and that experience gives a living Christ, who leads ever onward those who will adventure with Him, and not a prophet of the past, whose words might pass into a dead tradition.

At the same time, the indwelling Christ is continuous with the Man who died; and Paul clearly assumes a knowledge of the Jesus of the Gospels in his correspondents. It is probable, in fact, that our earliest Gospel took form to meet the needs of the new Churches of the Gentile Mission, and that the Gospel according to Luke represents the picture of Jesus Christ which was given to the Pauline Churches by

one who had worked for years under Paul's own direction. At the same time, we must say that Paul's service
to Christianity might have been even greater than it
was if he had given clear expression to the *direct* religious value of the life that Jesus lived. One of the
tasks still awaiting Christian thought is the filling out
of the categories of Pauline theology from the content
of the human life of Jesus. The Christian of this generation, to which modern scholarship has given a clearer
picture, perhaps, of Jesus of Nazareth than has been
possessed by men since the earliest ages of Christianity,
should steep his mind in the stories and sayings of the
Gospels, until the Figure of Jesus stands before him
in the colours of life, and then turn anew to the glow-
ing language in which Paul tells what that Figure
meant for him and means for all men. So we shall
miss neither the vivid humanity of the Gospel story
nor the splendid universality of Paul's vision of
Christ—the unseen Companion of humanity on its
long pilgrimage, who for the accomplishment of His
high mission wrought in a human life the critical act
of deliverance.

To the consideration of that act of deliverance we
must now turn.

VIII

THE DECISIVE BATTLE

It will be well at this point to recall the view which Paul sets before us of the situation with which Christ came to deal. Humanity was fighting a losing battle against Sin. For Sin had laid claim to the whole range of man's physical and psychical existence. The "inner man" maintained a feeble protest, especially where it was fortified by a clear knowledge of Right as expressed in law. But that protest did not make itself effective in action, for knowledge of the Law could not of itself overcome the weakness of the "flesh." So complete was the social and racial degradation of mankind that no individual born could escape partaking in the general wrongness, consciously or unconsciously. In either case the wrong way of life must lead to disaster—"The Wrath," or inevitable Nemesis of Sin in a moral universe. To meet the need, a way must be found to break the power of Sin and secure for man a new moral competence, and at the same time to replace the revelation of Right in terms of law by one which should establish personal relations congruous with the real character of God. There will therefore be two sides to the work of Christ, a negative or backward-looking, and a positive or forward-looking. On the one hand He must defeat Sin and clear scores with Law. On the other hand He must bring man moral power and create in him a principle of self-determined goodness. These two aspects of the matter cannot always be clearly distinguished, for they are complementary at every stage; but we may say roughly that the one side is represented by what is called the doctrine of Justification by Faith, the other by the even more important Pauline teaching about life "in Christ." We consider first the former aspect of the matter.

In order to understand Paul's teaching here it is necessary to give full weight to his belief in the solidarity of man. On the one side that solidarity is considered as "forensic," i.e. mankind is regarded as a real corporation which acts and suffers in the person of its representative. In primitive society the "personality" of the tribe or other community is so much more clearly defined than that of the individuals composing it that the whole community naturally suffers for any crime of one of its members. If an Achan breaks *tabu*, his whole kin must perish. If a Macdonald of Glencoe delays to take the oath of allegiance, his whole clan must be massacred. It is only an extension of that idea when Paul thinks of the human race as a corporation represented on the natural plane by "Adam," the hypothetical ancestor, whose act of sin involves the whole Race; but capable also of being represented by Christ, and sharing likewise in His "act of righteousness." [1] On the other hand the solidarity is considered as metaphysical. "Flesh," or the lower part of human nature, is thought of as a *continuum*, in which all individual men share. It is a tainted heritage which comes to each man burdened with the results of racial sin. Thus a blow struck at Sin by any human being who partakes of the "flesh" is struck on behalf of all.

On this double idea of human solidarity rests the

theoretical exposition of Paul's thought about the work of Christ. It is clear that for the purpose of his doctrine the reality of Christ's human life is absolutely demanded. Only a real man of flesh and blood could strike the blow for all men. God, says Paul, sent His Son "in the form of sinful flesh." The word "form" is not to be taken as expressing any unreality. By taking "flesh," Christ occupied the post of danger, for Sin was lord of the flesh, and claimed Him as its slave. That He successfully resisted that claim is the gift He gave to all men who are partakers with Him of our common nature. He was not a sinner in His own person; but "God made Him sin for us." That is said from the point of view rather of the "forensic" doctrine of solidarity. Jesus was made the representative of sinful man, and so before the law was responsible for sin. We have now an elaborate metaphor of a law-suit. Sin (personified) claimed its slave, but the verdict was given against the plaintiff. That, and not merely the moral censure of sin, is meant by the strange phrase that "God condemned Sin in the flesh." The claim of Sin upon Christ was disallowed, and therefore the claim of Sin upon all men who are identified with Christ was disallowed. His death, which might seem a victory for Sin, is shown by the following resurrection not to be such a victory. Death had not touched Christ's real self; it had become, instead of final defeat, a passage out of the bondage of "flesh" into the "liberty of the Spirit." "The death He died, He died in relation to Sin, once for all; the life that He lives, He lives in relation to God." [2]

In all this, Christ is the representative of a corporation which potentially includes all humanity. Those who are made one with Christ by that act of "faith," which we shall presently consider more particularly, enter at once into the benefits of this emancipation from Sin and this liberty of the Spirit. It is very clearly to be observed that Christ's action is throughout strictly representative. He acts for us, but not in a sense which excludes us from the act, but rather includes us in it. "One died for all; therefore all died," says Paul quite clearly. And when he comes to expound the matter in more detail, he shows that this co-operation in the act, however "forensically" it is conceived, is to be interpreted in a very practical way. "He died for all, so that those who live should no longer live for themselves." In fact, Christ's action becomes available for men exactly in proportion as His representation of them becomes a real thing, that is in proportion as they accept its implications, and make them the guiding principles of their own lives.[3]

It is surely in a similar sense that we must understand the metaphor of sacrifice, which has been pressed so exclusively in much Christian theology, though so far as Paul is concerned it is less akin to his habitual ways of thought than the metaphor of the lawsuit. The practice of sacrifice is in one form or another characteristic of all religions in their earlier stages of development. The meanings given to it are various, but almost all depend upon the idea of solidarity in some sense. The victim is often considered as one with the Deity, and the worshippers by partaking in the sacrifice are admitted to the same unity. The sacrificing priest acts in a completely representative capacity: his act is the act of the body of worshippers, and the benefits of the act accrue to them all. Again, in many forms of ancient sacrifice the priest so represented the Deity that he was considered as identical with the Deity, and so also with the victim he offered. Deity, victim, priest, and worshippers formed in the act of sacrifice an organic whole. Just how much of this complex of ideas lay explicitly in the minds of the people to whom Paul wrote it is impossible to say; but such is the background of the most universal element in the religions of his time. It has indeed been well observed that to the ancients it seemed that they had told the inmost secret of a matter when they had expressed it in terms of sacrifice, whereas for us it is just there that the difficulty begins.

We may find a clue to the idea which for Paul was most regulative of the meaning of sacrifice in the exhortation which he addressed to his correspondents at Rome: "Offer your bodies as a living sacrifice, holy and fit for God's acceptance, for this is the worship which reason renders." [4] To give the sentence its proper tone we may recall that by "body" Paul meant the whole personality, and not merely the structure of flesh and blood. Sacrifice is therefore first of all the dedication to God of all that one has and is. It is surely of this sacrifice that he speaks when he uses that old-world expression "the blood of Christ." For to the ancient mind "the life thereof is the blood thereof." [5] The shedding of blood meant the laying down of the life. And this laying down of the life derives its full significance from the thought of solidarity. An ancient prophet had drawn from the thought of solidarity the splendid conception of an ideal Servant of the Lord who would surrender his life in all manner of humiliation and suffering that others might live. "Thou shalt make his life an offering for sin. . . . By his knowledge shall My righteous Servant justify many." [6] It seems to have been in that thought that Jesus went to His death. Paul did not regard this self-sacrifice of Christ as being altogether different in kind from the self-sacrifice to which all Christian people are called in their way. He professed himself ready "to make up the deficit of Christ's sufferings on behalf of His Body, the Community." [7] But there was a completeness about the self-dedication of Christ which, like everything about Him, pointed to a unique relation to the universal action and eternal purpose of God for and in man, and which certainly proved itself decisive in its historical results. The sacrifice of Jesus Christ takes its unique significance from what He was. The ethical basis of it all is most clearly brought out by Paul. "Just as the transgression of a single individual issued in condemnation for all men, so the *righteous act* of a single individual issued for all men in a setting-right ('justification'), which brought (new) life. For as through the disobedience of one man the multitude of men were set wrong, so by the *obedience* of the one the multitude will be set right." [8]

In the light of all this we may read the passage in which Paul most explicitly sets forth the work of Christ in sacrificial terms:

All went wrong and missed the divine splendour; and all are set right by God's free grace through the emancipation worked in the person of Jesus Christ. God set Him forth as a means of annulling sin, through the trust (of men), in virtue of the laying-down of His life. This God did to show His righteousness, because of His passing-over of former wrongdoings while He held His hand—with a view to showing His righteousness at the present time, so that He might be at once righteous and the Setter-right of those who take their stand upon trust in Jesus. [9]

On this difficult passage two comments in particular must be made. First, the word which our familiar version gives as "propitiation" does not mean propitiation, which is properly the soothing of an angry person. The noun *hilasterion* is derived from the verb *hilaskesthai,* and means an instrument or means for the accomplishment of the action indicated by the verb. The original meaning of *hilaskesthai* is "to soothe an angry person." [10] In the Greek Old Testament, for example, it is so used for Jacob's propitiation of Esau. But while pagan usage frequently makes God the object of such an act, this idea is suggested in the Old Testament by only three passages out of some scores, and nowhere in the New Testament. [11] On the other hand, the meaning "to expiate or annul sin or defilement," which is also found in the pagan use of the term, becomes the regular meaning in the Old Testament. The subject may be a man (such as a priest), or God. In the former case the reference may be to sacrifice, or to ritual washing, or to any such act by which it was believed in ancient times that uncleanness could be removed. In the latter case, the meaning is equivalent to "forgive." [12] In our present passage, though God is not actually made the subject of the verb "to expiate," yet He is said to have "set forth a means of expiation," or of dealing with sin. The means is shown to be thought of in sacrificial terms by the following mention of "blood," in the sense of life laid down. So far, therefore, from the sacrifice of Christ being thought of as a means of soothing an angry Deity, it is represented as an act of God Himself to cope with the sin which was devastating human life.

The other comment is upon the latter part of the passage, and may be made more shortly by a reference to what has been said above (p. 76). "The passing-over of former wrong-doings" means the exhibition, in religious experience, of a principle of the divine healing which is inconsistent with strict law. Under the old régime, as Paul sees it, there were two different principles at work, the principle of retribution embodied in the scheme of things, and the principle of mercy discerned in the personal dealings of God with men. What was called for was a new revelation in which one single principle of righteousness should be displayed, and God's character be fully shown forth in dealing with human sin.[13] This was accomplished in God's gift of Christ, and in that act of self-dedication to which His "obedience" to God led him.

There is nothing here about a penalty borne by Christ as a substitute for guilty man. The nearest Paul comes to such a suggestion is in a passage in the

Epistle to the Galatians where he uses the metaphor
of the "curse." [14] To the thought of the ancient
world the curse was a real force launched upon the
world and destined ultimately to work itself out. Such
was the curse that lay upon the House of Atreus in
Greek legend, and such the curse pronounced upon
Babylon by the Hebrew prophets. Now the Law pronounced a curse upon all who should break it. Such a
curse must fulfil itself, quite mechanically. It is a good
argumentum ad hominem, at least, when Paul, writing to the half-Greek, half-Anatolian, and wholly superstitious people of the Galatian province, bids them
think of Christ as having exhausted in His own person the venom of the ancient curse—somewhat as Ores-
tes in the Greek legend exhausted the curse of the
House of Atreus and finally "reconciled" the Furies
who pursued the family. The teachers who were seeking to bring Paul's converts back into the allegiance
of the Jewish Law said that unless they complied at
least with certain minimum requirements, the Law
still had power to condemn them. Paul replies:
"Even supposing the sentence of the Law to have
all the inevitable potency you attribute to a solemn
curse, yet such a curse can be exhausted. Now Christ
bore that curse; for He was crucified, and the Law
expressly puts under a curse the crucified person. Yet
He survived it, and came out victorious. He must
therefore have broken the power of the curse, and
you need fear the Law no more." In so far as this is
more than metaphor, it is meaningless to us, for we
do not believe that a curse is a substantive force
working inevitably. But we do believe, because we see
it actually happen, that there are circumstances in
which, by defying the consequences, a person may so
endure the pain of corporate wrongdoing as to win
power to lead his fellows out of it. In that sense the
comparison throws a real light upon the work of
Christ. It is, however, only a passing illustration which

occurred to Paul in the midst of that particular controversy, and he does not return to it in later letters.

More might be said of the various figures and
forms of thought in which Paul embodies his conviction of the decisive value of the work of Christ. To
our ways of thought his whole construction is not very
satisfactory, if it be treated in any sense as a system
of theology. But by the flashes of light he throws here
and there we can partly re-read what he tries to por-
tray. Jesus Christ took the full risk of the human fight
against wrong. He accepted honestly and fearlessly all
the conditions of human nature, and in the wilderness,
on the mountain, in the garden, and in those countless "temptations" of which He spoke to His disciples, he faced the common foe. He faced it as one
"born of woman," having in his human nature the
conditions which in us all make for sin. He faced it as
one "born under the Law," that is as a Jew of His
time, whose temptations took the specific forms
proper to His age and country. What is more, He
faced it as one who deliberately threw in His lot with
the sinful and weak. He did not withdraw Himself
or stand aloof, but was content to be known as the
companion of disreputable characters. All this we
know to be true of the actual life of Jesus Christ. And
facing in this way our common battle, He won victory
all along the line. He accepted life in a spirit of utter self-dedication—of what Paul calls a "living sacrifice"—and He carried it right through to death;
death with every circumstance of horror, and with
every chance of escaping it almost to the very end, at
the cost of the smallest unfaithfulness.

But what has all this ancient history to do with us?
We should scarcely accept Paul's ways of stating solidarity. We do know, however, that solidarity is very
real. We are in large measure the product for good
and ill of the racial history which lies behind us, and
of the social environment into which we are born. The

mystery of heredity is not yet solved; but certainly since man had a mental life or "psychology," that psychology has been social as well as individual, and it comprises factors, present in the individual, which are due to the experience of the race, and most of all to the achievements of its leaders. The champions of a nation's liberties, to take an example, bequeath to their nation more than the actual constitutional liberties they secure in black and white: they form a psychology of liberty into which every member of that nation is born. He must do something with it; he may disown and struggle against it, but he cannot divorce his life from its influence. The same is true of the great witnesses to truth, and the great lovers of men—the poets and artists in life, to whose music the chords of every individual soul within their corporate tradition are strung, whether they are played upon or not. So it is that on a universal human scale what Christ did He did for us. His great fight and victory are part of the spiritual history of the Race, into which we are all born. We react one way or another to those decisive facts. They happened, and they exist today as an indelible part of the psychological heritage of man. The world in which Christ died is not a world in which one can live without meeting at all points, in oneself and in one's environment, the moral challenge and the moral possibilities which that event mingled in the stuff of our history. We may react differently to them. One will accept Christ's way, thereby laying himself open to all the divine forces, working within humanity, which Christ released. Another will reject His way, and thereby make himself an alien from this main stream of spiritual progress. In either case, the acceptance or rejection is not a theoretical attitude to a dim past, but a daily reaction to forces "in the air" of the world in which we move from day to day. Society is still a tangle of conflicting forces; we throw our lives into the sphere of *these* forces or of *those*. To be a Christian is to fling oneself without reserve into the stream of forces issuing from Christ's supreme moral achievement.

When we take this point of view, there are certain elements in the life and death of Jesus Christ which are seen at once to be decisive for us all. He greeted God as Father and Friend in everything and at every point. His life was that of a Son, and it was as a Son of God that He made His sacrifice of self-dedication to the Father. Towards His fellows a love such as He discerned in God was the perpetual motive power of action—a love generous, impartial, uncalculating, passionate to save—a love that put active, unceasing beneficence to the "neighbor" in the central place, and met wrong with an overplus of good. In such a life, the principle of sonship and of freedom from retributive Law is made manifest, and so the possibility of a new kind of life is communicated to man.

A word should here be spoken upon the significance which Paul attaches to the resurrection of Christ as the consummation of His work. It is true that for him, and certainly for us, the resurrection is vastly more important as the condition of that permanent communion with Christ which is the center of the new life. Of this much more will be said presently. But Paul also sees in it the conclusive proof of His victory over Sin. For us it can hardly take the same place it took for him in precisely this relation, if only because bodily death has not for us the same intimate connection with Sin that Paul had been taught to attribute to it.[15] We see in death something quite natural, and not necessarily horrible. Yet in the fact that death had, manifestly, no power to quench the living activity of Jesus Christ we may see a pledge that the natural order itself is subordinate to the ends of the spiritual life. In that order the death of the body is an episode, of much interest and significance indeed, but still only an episode, for those who stand for what Christ stood for—which is in the end what the Universe stands for. Putting it negatively, we might say: Suppose Christ, having lived as He did live and died as He did die, had then simply gone under. Suppose no one had henceforward had any sense of dealing with Him. Suppose in particular that that great wave of spiritual experience had not passed over the primitive Christians, assuring them that their Lord was in their midst, and making a Church possible. Suppose all this to be true: it would not necessarily destroy the validity of what Christ stood for; but it might leave us asking whether perhaps He was a mere rebel against a universe which, on the whole, stood for something quite different. There are many who do think so. They are our allies in the great fight, but they are apt to be depressing allies. If, on the other hand, we hold the continued personal existence and activity of Jesus Christ to be an assured fact, then we know that what He wrought on our behalf is also wrought into the very fabric of the universe in which we live; and we are at home in it, even while we rebel against its wrongs.

IX

EMANCIPATION

The death of Jesus Christ, then, we shall consider as a decisive fact not only in past history, but in the present constitution of man's world of thought and action, a fact towards which we must needs take up an attitude positive or negative. It was the crisis of a great conflict. The forces of evil gathered themselves for a decisive assault upon the moral integrity of the Son of God. They drove Him through the horror of failure, scorn, agony of mind and body, dereliction of soul, and death in darkness. For all the storm He never bent or broke. It did not change His perfect self-surrender to God, or the purity of His love to those who wrought the wrong. Therein was the proof of His victory. Such is the fact to which we have to orientate ourselves. We may decline to accept for ourselves what Christ did; we may refuse the principle which His life and death carried to victory. If so, then we assert against Christ the contrary principle, the principle which slew Him. "Saul, Saul, why persecutest thou Me?" is the protest which Christ utters against our action. On the other hand, we may accept the principle of what Christ did. We may accept it, not as those who believe themselves fit and "able to drink of that cup, and with that baptism to be baptized," but as those who are willing that the act and mind of God so revealed should be the principle of their own lives, and will leave the shaping of those lives to Him. This is what Paul calls "faith."

This conception is of such fundamental importance in Paul's teaching that we must try to understand it more particularly. In the theological constructions which have been based upon Paul the term "faith" has suffered such twistings and turnings that it has almost lost definition of meaning. Indeed, even in Paul's own use of the word there is very great complexity. Perhaps, however, we may get a clue from his use of the familiar words "faith to remove mountains." The expression echoes a saying of Jesus Christ; and we shall not go far wrong in starting from the use Jesus made of the word. "Have faith in God" was the one condition He propounded to those who sought His help.[1] By that is clearly meant trust, confidence directed towards God as the Father and Friend of men. This is the meaning of the word to Paul.[2] As it is Christ who not only shows us the God in whom we trust, but who has also Himself cleared away obstacles and made such trust possible, faith is alternatively described as "the faith of Christ," or "faith towards Christ." [3] That, however, is for Paul in no way different from faith in God. God is in the last resort the object of faith, for "God is trustworthy." That is the fundamental postulate of Paul's belief: God is worthy of our trust.[4] It remains for us to trust Him sufficiently to let Him act. It is wrong to suppose that for Paul faith is a meritorious act on man's part, which wins salvation, or even, in a more modern way of speech, a creative moral principle in itself. Paul does not, in fact, speak when he is using language strictly, of "justification *by* faith," but of "justification by grace through faith," or "on the ground of faith." [5] This is not mere verbal subtlety. It means that the "righteousness of God" becomes ours, not by the assertion of the individual will as such, but by the willingness to let God work. The critical moment in the religious life, according to Paul, is the moment when one is willing to "stand still and see the salvation of God." We can see how he came upon that thought. Paul had supposed that he was securing "righteousness" by a life of feverish activity, self-assertive, competitive, violent. It all did nothing but involve him more deeply in moral impotence. Then he was struck down. "Lord, what wilt Thou have me to do?" was the confession of surrender, the word of "faith."

Naked I wait Thy love's uplifted stroke.
My armour piece by piece Thou hast hewed from me.
I am defenceless utterly.

Such is the tone of saving faith in God. It is surrender. As related to Jesus Christ, it is expressed in the saying "I am crucified with Christ"—or at least that is part of the meaning of those pregnant words. For the cross of Christ manifests utter self-abandonment to the will of God. When Paul sought to recall his Galatian converts to the full meaning of their faith, he reminded them how he had "depicted Christ crucified before their eyes," and that had inspired their surrender to God.[6]

This trust in God is, Paul says, the ground of our "justification," or "setting-right." The word is in the first place a term of the law-courts. Much as we are said to "justify" a course of action when we show it to be the right course, a judge was said to "justify" a man when he pronounced him, upon the evidence, innocent of any crime laid to his charge, and so restored him to his rights as a citizen. Here, therefore, we have one of a whole series of religious and ethical terms which were inherited from Judaism with its legal outlook. For the later Jews morality was a legal obligation to be met; sin was a "debt," forgiveness a "remission" of the legal penalty. Along with these terms goes the word "justification," meaning the acquittal of an accused person. It must first be understood in its proper legal sense, with the help of the entire setting of the law-court, and then as the whole of ethics is translated out of legal into personal terms, "justification" will be translated with the rest. Paul's whole work is a standing challenge to make such a translation complete.

Here then we have the human soul a prisoner at the bar of ideal righteousness—its own thoughts accusing and defending, as Paul says.[7] The verdict on the facts must be "Guilty": there can be no other. No soul is clear from personal participation in the moral evil of the race. That verdict carries with it the sentence to go on sinning till moral disaster ensues; for the Wrath or Nemesis of sin is that man is left to his own evil propensities. The sin we have admitted into our life is self-propagating, for "what a man sows, he reaps." [8] But now the prisoner makes his appeal: "I confess myself guilty, a slave of sinful habit. Nevertheless I disown this sinful self. I accept the act of Christ, as representing me. He died to sin; I make His act mine. I am crucified with Christ, and I throw myself in trust upon the God whom Christ has shown me."

> "I bind unto myself to-day . . .
> By power of faith, Christ's incarnation . . '
> His death on Cross for my salvation,
> His rising from the spiced tomb,
> His riding up the heavenly way." [9]

On that basis the prisoner is acquitted. The process cannot be understood apart from the antique idea of solidarity which has already been explained. The accused is acquitted, not by virtue of a righteousness individually achieved by him, but by virtue of the

righteousness of his representative which he accepts
as his own in the act of faith. "The righteous act of
one issues in justification for all . . . through the
obedience of one the multitude are set right." [10] There
is no thought of a penalty borne by a substitute,
but only of a righteousness achieved by a representative.

So far it would seem that the transaction is a legal
fiction. To an ancient, indeed, its fictitious character
would scarcely be obvious, since for him representation was a fact, and not a fiction. For us, however, if
this is all there is to be said, then the doctrine of justification is unreal. But this is not all. We now approach the translation from legal into personal terms.
What is the actual state of mind of the "justified"
person? He has disowned, not merely certain evil
practices, but his own guilty self. That is implied in
the act of faith in Christ. He is crucified with Christ.
So far as the whole intention of his mind is concerned, that guilty self is dead and done with. The
controlling factor in the situation is the power and
love of God as revealed in Christ and His "righteous
act." That is the center about which the man's whole
being moves in the moment of "faith." Outwardly,
he is the same man he was, open still to his neigh-
bors' harsh judgment, liable still to condemnation
under a law which balances achievement against
shortcoming. But really the man is changed through
and through by that act of self-committal, self-abandonment to God. Before God he is indeed dead to
sin and alive in a quite new way to righteousness. In
fact, he is righteous, in a fresh sense of the word; in a
sense in which righteousness is no longer, so to say,
quantitative, but qualitative; in which it consists not
in a preponderant balance of good deeds achieved,[11]
but in a comprehensive attitude of mind and will. If
our highest values are personal values, then at bottom
a man is right or wrong according to his relation with

the personal center of reality, which is God. There is
only one such relation which is right, and that is the
relation of trusting surrender to God. A man who is in
that relation to God is right. He is justified, in no fictitious way, but by the verdict of reality. He possesses
righteousness—"not a righteousness of my own, resting
upon law, but the righteousness which comes through
trust in Christ, (or to put it differently) the righteousness which comes from God on the condition of
trust." [12]

There is a real moral and religious revolution here.
A legal religion lays all the emphasis on what a man
does, or wills to do. The power of the will, the self-
assertive element in us, is brought into the foreground. In direct contrast to this is the religion which
says that not what we do, but what God does, is the
root of the matter. "It is not a matter of deeds done,
lest anyone should boast." [13] Righteousness is not the
offering of sacrifice, the doing of good deeds, the entertaining of right opinions, or any of the things
whereby the self is asserted. It is the quiet acceptance
of that working of God whereby we are saved. "It is
good that a man should both trust and quietly wait for
the Lord." The immense energy of the religious life is
rooted in a moment of passivity in which God acts.
There is, in fact, no ultimate deliverance from sin
apart from this. If every man started his course with
a clean sheet and a perfectly free will, things might
be different. But none of us do so start. Our best efforts at self-reform are tainted and misdirected by the
evil that is in us. That is why so often the most sincere efforts of religious men have produced the most
disastrous results. The more fervour and energy they
throw into their endeavours, the worse for society. The
author of Ecclesiastes had this kind of righteousness
in mind when he gave the caution "Be not righteous
overmuch." Paul knew about it, for he had, in the
fervour of his religious zeal, been a persecutor. But

on the Damascus road he came to a standstill; and in that moment a new creation was effected. The weight of past evil was gone: a new life, God-directed, began.

How immense the moral task which this new creation imposes we shall presently see. For the moment let us contemplate the significance of this revolution in religion. The higher faiths call their followers to strenuous moral effort. Such effort is likely to be arduous and painful in proportion to the height of the ideal, desperate in proportion to the sensitiveness of the conscience. A morbid scrupulousness besets the morally serious soul. It is anxious and troubled, afraid of evil, haunted by the memory of failure. The best of the Pharisees tended in this direction, and no less the best of the Stoics. And so little has Christianity been understood that the popular idea of a serious Christian is modelled upon the same type of character. There is little joy about such a religion; and as any psychologist can tell us, the concern about evil magnifies its power. The ascetic believed that because he was becoming so holy the Devil was permitted special liberties with him, and found in his increasing agony of effort a token of divine approval. Not along this track lies the path of moral progress. Christianity says: Face the evil once for all, and disown it. Then quiet the spirit in the presence of God. Let His perfections fill the field of vision. In particular let the concrete embodiment of the goodness of God in Christ attract and absorb the gaze of the soul. Here is righteousness, not as a fixed and abstract ideal, but in a living human person. The righteousness of Christ is a real achievement of God's own Spirit in man. It is a permanent and growing possession of humanity. It is historic and integral to our world. Let that righteousness be the center of attention, and the only movement of the soul a full consent to God from whom it all proceeds. When that is so, the morbid cleft between the soul and its ideal is bridged; the insidious haunting presence of sin is banished; new powers invade the soul. "It is God who is at work in us, both in act and in will." [14]

It is perhaps worth while to add that modern psychologists recognize the importance of passivity or self-surrender as the means to a renewal of life and energy. "Weakness results from the wastage caused by restlessness of mind; Power comes from a condition of mental quietude," says one of them, adding that "several of the greatest psychologists . . . have tended towards the view that the source of power is to be regarded as some impulse that works through us, and is not of our own making." [15] Another observes that "to exercise the personal will is still to live in the region where the imperfect self is the thing most emphasized. Where, on the contrary, the subconscious forces take the lead, it is more probably the better self *in posse* that directs the operation." Accordingly a person "must relax, that is, he must fall back on the larger Power that makes for righteousness.[16]

We must now observe that this experience of "justification" assumes a different aspect according as the point of view is specifically religious or specifically ethical. Religious experience has about it something which is timeless or eternal. In the moment of the soul's touch with God the time process disappears. Hence "justification" as a pure religious experience of the grace of God is complete in itself and eternal in its value. Paul can speak of it historically as if for the Christian it was an event finished once for all.[17] But, on the other hand, no one has more cogently than he presented the tremendous moral endeavour to live out the righteousness of God. From this ethical point of view, to which the time-process is all-important, righteousness is a gradual attainment. Almost at the very end of his life Paul could write, "It is not as though I had already won, or become perfect; I am pressing on in the hope that I may lay hold of that for which Christ Jesus laid hold of me. My brothers, I do not reckon that I have laid hold of it yet; but there is one thing—I do forget all that lies behind, and stretch out to what lies before, and I press on towards the mark, for the prize of God's upward call in Christ Jesus." [18] One who spoke in that way can hardly be accused of neglecting the progressive element in morality. Yet Paul is never far from the thought of that finished work from which all human endeavour flows. "Work out your own salvation, *because* it is God who is at work in you." [19]

There is a difficulty here for us, as it proved a difficulty for his first converts. It may be that the peculiar character of his own conversion—its suddenness and completeness—may have led him into too unqualified statements of the "once-for-all-ness" of justification. In any case it is clear that he was misunderstood on this point by converted pagans who took in unintelligent literalness his strong assertion that "we have been cleansed, justified, sanctified." We cannot, however, escape from the difficulty by any short cut. There *is* a finality in that religious experience which Paul calls justification, while there is none the less a moral process. For most of us there must be a repeated harking back to the moment of surrender. After failure and fall we must enter once more into the "secret place of the Most High" to renew our abnegation of the guilty self and our acceptance of the righteousness of God in Christ. Paul perhaps allows too little for this necessity, explicitly at least. But for all that, it is of vital importance that he told us so plainly that everything depends on an act of God, eternal and single, in the soul, renewable indeed by acts of faith, but in its essence the one abiding fountain of all such acts, as of all moral endeavour.

"God justifies the ungodly." [20] That is the watchword of the Pauline Gospel. It states in a dogmatic phrase the truth which the life of Jesus declared. To the paralytic He pronounced forgiveness, there and then, before any amendment or reparation of wrong had taken place, simply on the ground of faith. The woman who was a sinner He accepted as forgiven, finding the proof of it in the love she showed. He received disreputable characters. No Pharisee would have objected, one supposes, if He had first made them respectable and then consorted with them. The Pharisees could do not away with this restoration to full rights as children of God on the sole ground of a simple faith. To forgive the paralytic was "blasphemy"; to receive sinners was a scandal. But Jesus told a story of two men who went to pray. The disreputable tax-collector threw himself on the mercy of God in simple trust. He went home "justified." The Pharisee thanked God for the righteousness he had attained—as Paul would say, "he gloried before God on the ground of works." But he was not justified. One Pharisee at least awoke to the truth, and he has told us what it meant. It took a Pharisee to see all that Christ's action implied. Paul the Pharisee put it into the crabbed theological terms he had been taught, but transcended those terms in the statement.

It will help towards the appreciation of what Paul meant by the forensic term "justification" if we consider other figures which he uses to describe the same experience. It is emancipation, deliverance from the yoke of an external moral standard and from the tyranny of evil habit. The justified man is like a slave freed from his master's power; or like a widow whom her husband's death has emancipated from the absolute dominion (*potestas*) into which Roman Law gave the married woman; or like the heir who on attaining his majority bids farewell to guardians and trustees, and becomes master in his own house.[21] It is no mere change of status of which Paul speaks in such metaphors. It is a real deliverance from something which denies free play to the human will to good. Yet it is not the attainment of that "unchartered freedom" which means bondage to "chance desires." [22] On the other side, it means entering into a new allegiance. Once Paul describes it, apologizing for the boldness of the metaphor, as "servitude" towards God. And indeed his perpetual use of the appellation "slave of Jesus Christ," which is directly correlative to the title "Lord," preserves always the sense of a very binding allegiance. The immediate antecedents of language of that kind are probably to be found in the religious terminology of the time. The members of a religious cult, bound sacramentally to one another and to their patron God, addressed Him as their "Lord." The Emperor was addressed as "Lord" when he was regarded as a divine object of worship. It was because the Christian would not give the Emperor the divine honour which he retained for Jesus alone, that the Church came into deadly conflict with the Empire. Thus Paul thought of the Christian life as freedom within a very absolute allegiance.

The more pregnant term, however, for this relation to God is "sanctification." In religious language "holy" means devoted to the Deity. The sanctification of the Christian means that he is entirely devoted to God; he is as truly and exclusively dedicated to the service of God as any temple or priest in the older religions. The distinction which theology has made between justification as the momentary act of deliverance and sanctification as the process of attaining perfection is not to be found in Paul. For him they are only different aspects of the same act.[23] By the same act of grace that justifies we are also sanctified; and as the righteousness attributed to us by the act of justification is to be appropriated through a course of moral endeavour, so is the sanctity imparted to us by the same act to be worked out in the moral life. God justifies the ungodly, and in the same sense He sanctifies the unholy. He claims us as entirely His own; and in proportion as we admit that claim steadily in all the changing experiences of life, it establishes itself in a character bearing the manifest stamp of God.

We are already at the point of transition from what has been called the negative or backward-looking aspect of Christ's work for us to the positive or forward-looking. The two aspects are combined by Paul in one striking and comprehensive metaphor, that of dying and rising again. Here he makes use of the symbolism of baptism, which in the East was performed by the complete immersion of the believer in water. "We were buried with Christ through our baptism (and so entered) into a state of death, in order that, just as Christ was raised from the dead through the splendour of the Father, we too might walk in the newness which belongs to (real) life." [24] To the rite as such Paul did not attach overwhelming importance. "Christ," he says, "did not send me to baptize, but to preach the Gospel." [25] But to his pagan converts it appealed as a sacrament parallel to those of the Greek mysteries. The governing idea of all mysteries was that by the performance of physical acts spiritual effects could be attained. And principally, such sacramental acts united the worshipper with his dying and rising Saviour-God. In some cults such a union seems to have been regarded as a real dying and rising of the worshipper, in the sense that through the sacrament he acquired from the God an immortal essence. In a similar way Paul's pagan converts thought of baptism. Paul recognized in the idea a most suggestive figure for the change wrought by faith in Christ. He found it necessary to guard against the crude sacramentalism which found in the mere physical process as such the actual impartation of new life, quite apart from anything taking place in the realm of inward experience. The Israelites in the wilderness, he pointed out in a curious argument, received baptism in the Red Sea and in the cloud which overshadowed them; and yet

they were disobedient, "the majority of them God did
not choose," and they perished miserably.[26] The inference is plain. No sacramental act achieves anything
unless it is an outward symbol of what really happens inwardly in experience. The test of that is the
reality of the new life as exhibited in its ethical consequences. "How can we who are dead to sin live any
longer in sin?" If baptism is a real dying and rising
again, then it is indeed a profound revolution in the
personal life, a revolution which is simply bound to
show itself in a new moral character.

It is in this sense that Paul appeals to the baptism
of the Christian—the act by which he entered into the
Christian communion. If that rite means anything, he
says, it means that you share with Christ His dying to
sin and His rising to new life.

The death He died, He died in relation to sin, once
for all; the life He lives, He lives in relation to God.
In the same way you must reckon yourselves as dead in
relation to sin, and alive in relation to God in (communion with) Christ Jesus. And so Sin must not reign
in your mortal body (i.e. in the physical part of the
individual organism, in which, according to Paul, Sin
had become firmly entrenched) so that you obey its
desires. Do not make over your bodily organs to Sin,
as implements of unrighteousness, but make yourselves over to God, as persons raised to life from the
dead, and your bodily organs as implements of righteousness to Him. For Sin shall not be your lord, since
you are not under Law, but under (God's) grace.[27]

In reading the passage we are aware that Paul is
speaking of something profoundly real in his own
experience. We have left now the region of *mere*
metaphor, and entered into a sphere where spiritual
realities are described in terms not indeed adequate to
them, but coming as near as may be to direct expression. The "death" spoken of is a real deadening of
certain sides of the nature, a real privation of life and

energy on the part of evil propensities. "I am crucified
to the world." The crucified person—the man with
the hangman's rope about his neck, shall we say?—has
done with this world, its interests and concerns. It is
all over. The mind has become detached. Even so Paul
found that in the moment of his conversion he had
become detached from much which had before dominated him. That obstinate "covetousness" which the
contemplation of law had seemed only to strengthen
—the ambition, egoism, perhaps lust, which are
summed up in that word—was dried up from its
springs. He cared no more about the very things which
had been his greatest pride. "The things which used to
be gain to me," he wrote, "I have now reckoned so
much loss because of Christ. In fact, I reckon everything mere loss, because the knowledge of Christ Jesus
my Lord so far exceeds them all. On His account I
have actually suffered the loss of everything, and I
reckon it all mere refuse—so that I may gain
Christ." [28]

It is apparent that, stated in its absolute form, this
"death and resurrection" was not true of many of his
pagan converts. To them the "death" was ceremonial,
the "resurrection" a theoretical inference from it, and
the moral change had taken place only partially. That
is why, instead of the positive statement which
would seem to be required logically, he sometimes
gives an exhortation. "Let not Sin reign . . . Do not
make your bodies implements of unrighteousness."
He seems, indeed, to have found by experience the
necessity for greater emphasis on the *process*. "I have
been crucified with Christ," he wrote to the Galatians
in the height of his mission. It has been pointed out
that crucifixion is in any case a lingering death. But
in what is possibly his last letter he speaks of "getting conformed to His death"—a process not yet complete. Yet he knew always that everything was involved in that decisive moment. He died to sin once.

Thenceforward he "carried about in the body the dying of the Lord Jesus," and the course of life as it came day by day made the death more and more a reality in the workaday world.[29] More and more in those later days he was conscious that the real life he lived was a hidden life. "You died," he wrote to the Colossians from his Roman prison, "and your life lies hidden with Christ in God. When Christ, who is our life, is manifested, then we too shall be manifested with Him in splendour." [30] The "self behind the frontage," it has been observed, is in all of us something greater than the self of the shop-window which all the world can see.[31] For the Christian that secret self is perpetually nourished into greatness by inward communion with God in Christ.

> *As torrents in summer,*
> *Half-dried in their channels,*
> *Suddenly rise, tho' the*
> *Sky is still cloudless,*
> *For rain has been falling*
> *Far off at their fountains—*
> *So hearts that are fainting*
> *Grow full to o'erflowing,*
> *And they that behold it*
> *Marvel, and know not*
> *That God at their fountains*
> *Far off has been raining.*[32]

The faithful endeavour to keep open all the avenues between this hidden world and the world of every day is the way to what Paul means by "getting conformed to the death of Christ" and "knowing the power of His resurrection."

X

THE LORD THE SPIRIT

"God gives proof of His love for us in the fact that while we were still in the wrong Christ died for us. Much more then, now that we have been set right by means of His self-sacrifice, shall we be saved from the Wrath through Him. For if while we were enemies we were reconciled to God through the death of His Son, much more now that we are reconciled shall we be saved by means of His life." [1] In that repeated "much more" is much virtue. Theology has often represented Paul as though he were supremely or even solely interested in the death of Christ on the cross and the "Atonement" thereby effected. This is a somewhat ironical fate for one who showed so clearly that his eyes were set upon the risen Christ, and his thought returned gladly again and again to the wonder of the new life He gave. That positive gospel of the resurrection-life in Christ was an even greater thing to Paul than the doctrine of justification, important as this was in clearing the ground of all that cumbered the course. "If you are risen with Christ, seek the things that are above, where Christ is, on the right hand of God." Paul is always exultantly aware that as a Christian he is a new man, living in a new age. With Christ's resurrection the limits of the old order have been broken through. It is an age of miracle, in which nothing is too good to be true. The hope of the new age had often associated itself with a belief in the emancipation of the body from the limitations of physical existence. Manifestly this had not come about for the Christians of the first century: they still looked for it to come at the Lord's appearing. But Paul held that in principle the Christian, whose real self was hid with Christ in God, was already delivered from the "flesh" and living in an age of "glory." The "flesh" might indeed be "an unconscionable time a-dying," but the actual experience of the new life showed that the moral powers of "eternal life" were at work.

Now in this Paul met half-way a characteristic belief of the pagan religious world. It was held possible, by the performance of certain rites, or the acquisition of certain secret knowledge, to become immortal while in the body. There was an inward "deification" which ensured everlasting life for the initiate after death. Paul made use of this idea, while correcting its exclusively metaphysical and sacramental bias. For the Greek—as indeed in large measure for later Christian theology as formed by the Greek mind—the essential thing was a change of "substance" or metaphysical nature; its means, a rite or an esoteric doctrine; and its aim and end the assurance of life beyond the grave. For Paul the essential thing was a new moral character, as the only real evidence of a life akin to the life of God, and its means was the receiving of Christ, not by any magical rite, nor by assent to a system of doctrine, but in the moral fellowship of "faith." The risen life is in the first place a life whose fruits are ethical. Prolonged into the future it means immortality, because life of that kind, made ethically valuable through a personal fellowship, cannot be ended by the death of the body.

Moral conduct and immortality alike are represented as the harvest of an indwelling Spirit. "The fruit of the Spirit is love, joy, peace, patience, kindness, goodness, loyalty, self-control"; "he who sows into the Spirit will reap out of the Spirit eternal life." Otherwise expressed, the Spirit is "the first instalment of our inheritance." All that man hopes for as the corporate perfection of life is given in principle by that Spirit whose moral efficacy is a matter of daily experience to the Christian.[2] This idea of the Spirit is so vital to Paul's teaching that it will be well to make some attempt to see it in its historical context of thought.

In Jewish apocalyptic thought, the expectation of "the life of the coming age," or the Kingdom of God, was associated with the idea of the possession of men by the divine, or holy, Spirit, which had moved the ancient prophets and saints. The possession of the Spirit was conceived as bringing a miraculous heightening of the normal powers—the ability to see things invisible, to hear divine voices, to speak mysterious and prophetic words, to heal disease, and to dominate the world of matter. After the death of Jesus there broke out among His followers phenomena such as have frequently been observed in periods of religious exaltation or "revival." Persons fell into trances in which they heard unutterable words spoken, or saw visions of Christ and of heavenly beings. The powers of suggestion and of suggestibility were greatly intensified, so that morbid cases of divided personality ("demon possession") yielded to the suggestions of sanity; and even physical ailments of the limbs and bodily organs proved amenable to treatment by mental processes. In public gatherings men would be moved by a storm of intense feeling to utter cries which, though inarticulate, were held to be full of deep meaning, perhaps even to be the "tongues of angels." On a higher level they had moments of exceptional insight into truth, which they attempted to express in words of "prophecy." [3] None of these phenomena were unparalleled or in the strict sense miraculous, but to the early Christians it seemed that these were the literal fulfilment of the miraculous expectations of Apocalyptic. They were valued accordingly, as the manifestation of the Messianic Spirit, the gift of the new age. The simple followers of Jesus to whom these strange things happened were elated by the sense of power they brought. They scarcely realized that the real miracle was something deeper and greater than all this. Beneath the froth of "revivalism" flowed the steady stream of moral life renewed through the inspiration of Jesus Christ in His life and death.

The Gospel went out into the pagan world, where the moral background of the original Christian community was lacking. The volatile converts of Anatolia and Greece hailed with avidity the most exciting and spectacular effects of the "revival" fervour. The magical and occult has always a fascination. There was grave danger that the Gospel would evaporate in a burst of sensationalism. This danger Paul had to face, and in facing it he was driven to apply the cold light of a searching criticism to these emotional phenomena in which he himself fully shared. The faculty of self-criticism is rare enough anywhere. It is particularly rare in enthusiasts. Paul possessed it, and for that reason he was able to give to the Christian community such a sympathetic and convincing estimate of spiritual values that the whole idea of the Spirit became a new thing. He never thought of denying that there was a real value in the visions of glory and the inspired utterances which men attributed to the Spirit; but he pointed out that these were mere symptoms, and symptoms of varying value. For instance, "speaking with tongues," or the utterance of emotional cries of no clear meaning, was, though more surprising,

far less valuable than the clear insight into truth
which expressed itself in prophecy. But greater than
all was the moral renewal that the Spirit brought. The
reality behind all was that sharing of the risen life of
Christ which reproduced in the believer the character
of his Lord.

We have seen that Paul believed in a "life-giving
Spirit" who all through the ages was the fountain of
life to men, and was manifested at last in an individual human person, Jesus Christ. In accordance with
this belief he held the Spirit, which the early Church
believed it possessed, to be no other than Christ Himself, now liberated from the necessary limitations of
His human life, and entering by direct fellowship into
the Christian. This did not mean, as has been said,
"a certain de-personalizing" of Christ. On the contrary, it meant the elevation of the idea of Spirit from
the category of substance to that of personality. To
have the Spirit does not mean, as it used to mean,
that some mysterious stream of divine essence is passing into the human organism. It means being in the
most intimate conceivable touch with a Person. There
are two sides to Christian experience as Paul knows it.
On the one side it is a life of trust and love towards
"the Son of God, who loved me and gave Himself for
me"; on the other side it is a life renewed from within
by an immanent Spirit. Yet the Lord we trust is none
other than the indwelling Spirit that is the inspirer of
our thoughts, our prayers, and our moral acts.[4] Christ
without, our Saviour, Friend, and Guide; Christ
within, the power by which we live.

There lies here a deep mystical experience only
partially capable of description in words. But is there
not a partly analogous duality in our deepest relations
with one another? You have a friend, dear as your
own soul, the very embodiment of that which you
admire and aspire to. Now you may sit in the room
and converse with your friend, and his spoken word,

or act, or look, may exert upon you the influence of
his personality. Or you may be apart and he may
exert that influence by letter. Or without letter you
may recall him so vividly that the memory serves as a
potent source of influence. All this is still the friend
without. But when once the influence is established,
there is a somewhat abiding in the central places of
your own mind which is yet not yours but your
friend's. You may even be unconscious of it, but it
shows itself in countless ways. Some one will remark,
"I seemed to hear X. in what you said just now"; or
"The way you did that was so exactly X. that I could
have fancied him here." In some strange way your
friend has become a part of yourself—*animæ dimi-
dium tuæ*. There is more here than we can readily
express; and perhaps it is not altgether different
from the double relation of Christ to the faithful soul.
Paul converses with the Lord as a man converses with
his friend: "Thrice I besought the Lord . . . and He
said . . ." But at other times "The Spirit of Jesus suffered him not." [5]

The Gospel used to be presented as an appeal to
believe in the Saviour who "did it all for me long
ago," and then retired to a remote heaven where He
receives the homage of believers till He come again to
inaugurate the Millennium. The mind of our generation, having little comprehension or taste for such a
message, is usually content to try and discover "the
Jesus of history," conceived as a human example and
teacher of a distant past. Meanwhile there exists always alongside all forms of religious belief the great
tradition of mystical experience. The mystic knows
that whatever be the truth about an historic act or
person there is a Spirit dwelling in man. In our time
even natural science abates its arrogant denials and
admits the possibility of such immanence. The most
deeply religious spirits of our time tend to take refuge
from the uncertainties of belief in an inward sense

of communion with the divine, which is too widely attested in human experience to be easily set aside; and they report that they have no need of an historic Christ at all. The weak point of mysticism, as seen at least by a matter-of-fact person, is that it is apt to be so nebulous ethically. What the Immanent is, those who claim most traffic with It can often tell us least. Is It a power making for righteousness, or is It a higher synthesis of good and evil? Or is It not a moral —that is to say, not a personal—Being at all? Does It work "by rapt æsthetic rote," "like a knitter drowsed"? [6] The raising of these questions is not intended to throw any doubt upon the validity of mystical experience as such; but we have a right to ask what content is given in the experience. Paul was a mystic, but all his mystical experience had a personal object. It was Jesus Christ, a real, living person —historic, yet not of the past alone; divine, yet not alien from humanity. The Spirit within was for him continuous with the Spirit of Jesus Christ, and recognized by His lineaments. To express this fact, Paul coined a new phrase. The primitive Christians were accustomed to speak, in language which was older than Christianity, of being "in the Spirit," as though Spirit were an ethereal atmosphere surrounding the soul, and breathed in as the body breathes the air. Paul, too, used this expression, but he placed alongside it a parallel form of words, "in Christ," or "in Christ Jesus." Where we find those words used we are being reminded of the intimate union with Christ which makes the Christian life an eternal life lived in the midst of time. The deeper shade of meaning would often be conveyed to our minds if we translated the phrase "in communion with Christ."

Thus the Imitation of Christ is not an attempt to copy His recorded acts and ways of life—an attempt which can scarcely expect much success, where the conditions of life are so different. It means to be "in

Christ," to give heed to the Christ within, who seeks
to propagate in other men the truly human life which
He once lived in Galilee and Jerusalem. The Christ
of Nazareth had one life only to live between the
manger and the cross—the life of Carpenter, Teacher,
and rejected Messiah of the Jews. He must live again
in countless human lives before He is fully Messiah
of mankind, in the lives of modern men and women
placed in a world so different from that which spread
itself around His village home in ancient Galilee. To
express this in a satisfying theology is a baffling task:
to make it a reality in life is a problem solved in sur-
prisingly large measure by many simple Christians in
all ages, who could say with Paul, "For me to live is
Christ." The truly Christian life is a life not tran-
scribed from the pages of the Gospels, but continuous
with the divinely human life there portrayed, because
the genius of the same Artist is at work on the new
canvas. "We all reflecting as in a mirror the splendour
of the Lord, are being transformed into the same image (of God), from splendour to splendour, as by the
working of the Lord the Spirit." [7]

We can trace how in Paul's writings this thought
of "the Lord the Spirit" dominated the whole range of
Christian experience. The initiation into the Christian
life—the baptism by which we die and rise again with
Christ—is "baptism in the Spirit," the steeping of the
whole being in the Spirit of Christ.[8] This is the true
baptism, of which the immersion in water is only the
effectual sign. It means the implanting within our human nature of a divine element, present indeed in
germ and in potentiality before, but woefully ob-
scured and frustrated by our participation in the
wrongness which infects all human society as it is.
This divine element, freed now and brought to conscious life, salutes the Lord and Giver of Life with
the acclamation "Abba, Father!" For the Spirit we
have received is the Spirit of the Son of God, and we

possessing it are God's sons too, and "that of God in us" leaps out towards the God who is the source of it. The Spirit of Jesus within us moves us to prayer: indeed, prayer is just that moving of God's Son in us towards the Father. Though we are burdened with the greatness of our need, so that our prayers are not even articulate, yet in such "inarticulate sighs" the Spirit "intercedes for us." This gives us the true character of all Christian worship. It is an expression of our "partnership with God's Son." [9] Whatever outward forms it may use—or shun—Christian worship is the reciprocal fellowship of God and His sons. He gives the Spirit, which then returns to Him in prayer and adoration. The norm and prototype is Christ the Son of God. The lonely prayers on Galilæan hills by night, the "exultation in the Spirit" when He cried "I thank Thee, Father, Lord of heaven and earth," the agonizing supplications of Gethsemane—"Abba, Father, Thy will be done!"—these are re-enacted in His brethren in whom the Spirit prays.

Therewith comes also a new possibility of knowledge of God. There is indeed a natural knowledge of God innate in man, but it is, in experience at least, dim and lacking in conviction, being mediated by His works.[10] But to share Christ's Spirit is to be admitted to the secrets of God. Perhaps one of the most striking features of the early Christian movement was the re-appearance of a confidence that man can know God immediately. Judaism had become traditional: the word of the Lord, the Rabbis held, came to the prophets of old, but *we* can only preserve and interpret the truth they handed down. Jesus Christ, with a confidence that to the timid traditionalism of His time appeared blasphemous, asserted that He knew the Father and was prepared to let others into that knowledge. He did so, not by handing down a new tradition about God, but by making others sharers in His own attitude to God. This is what Paul means by "having the mind of Christ." Having that mind, we do know God. It was this clear, unquestioning conviction that gave Paul his power as a missionary: but he expected it also in his converts. To them too "the word of knowledge" came "by the same Spirit." He prayed that God would give them a spirit of wisdom and revelation in the knowledge of Him. Such knowledge is, as Paul freely grants, only partial, but it is real, personal, undeniable knowledge.[11] In friendship between men there is a mutual knowledge which is never complete or free from mystery: yet you can know with a certainty nothing could shake that your friend is "not the man to do such a thing," or that such and such a thing that you have heard is "just like him." You have a real knowledge which gives you a criterion. Such is the knowledge the Christian has of his Father.

This knowledge of God gives a new ground for the ethical life. We have seen that for Paul the "conscience," or consciousness of oneself as a moral being, is the court of moral judgment. Now when a man has received the Spirit of Christ, that Spirit enters and inhabits the central place of his self-consciousness:[12] he is conscious of himself, not as a man merely, but as a son of God, standing in a special relation to Jesus Christ. When a moral question arises, it takes the form, not "Is this unworthy of myself? Does it hurt my self-respect?" but "Does this hurt my relation to Jesus Christ? Is it unworthy of Him?" Not that Jesus is referred to as an outside standard: it is "Christ living in me" who is the judge. In this way the Christian approaches all practical problems of ethics: he brings the mind of Christ to bear on it. This, of course, he cannot do unless the mind of Christ is his mind too. That is to say, the Christian solution of any difficulty cannot be reached by one who disinterestedly and externally examines and compares the evidence, without being committed to the result of his examination. It is revealed to him who lets Christ's mind dominate him day by day, and then sees things as they appear to that mind. He has thus his ethical standard within himself. Here is the real secret of moral emancipation. In the Gospels we see Jesus taking up a wonderfully detached attitude to traditional morality, picking and choosing, rejecting and sanctioning, in a way which must have appeared bewildering to his contemporaries—in a way, indeed, which few of His followers really understood. Paul grasped the secret of it. Jesus dealt in this sovereign way with the moral law because the Spirit of God who gave the law was His Spirit: because the inward impulse that shaped His own life was the very central impulse of all true morality. He was God's Son, and lived in His Father's house; and the law of the family of God was His very nature. In all this the Christian is a "partner of the Son of God." "He who has the Spirit judges all things, and is judged by no one." The principle of moral autonomy could not be more strenuously asserted.[13] And Paul's willingness to trust the autonomy of others is often really touching,[14] though we need not seek to excuse his occasional attempts at a dictation which was really not consistent with his principles.

Here we have Paul's sufficient justification against those who accused him of antinomianism or a relaxing of moral standards. The moral demand of letting Christ's Spirit rule you in everything is far more searching than the demand of any code, and at the same time it carries with it the promise of indefinite growth and development. It means that every Christian is a centre of fermentation where the morally revolutionary Spirit of Christ attacks the dead mass of the world. Ethical originality is the prerogative of the Christian whose conscience is the seat of Christ's indwelling: and such originality is imperative for a world which is "saved in hope," a world which needs progress. The seeming extreme individualism of this doctrine is corrected by the doctrine of the Body to which we shall come presently: but for the moment let us do full justice to Paul's claim of autonomy for the Christ-inspired conscience. It is a claim we must press with all our might in a world where belief in regimentation is strong and growing. In relation to the existing world-orders, in so far as they are based on the violent assertion of authority, serious Christianity is anarchism. It does indeed reverence authority in so far as that authority is "an agent of God for good," but it obeys God rather than man, and, in the last resort, with Paul, "cares not a rap for the judgment of any human tribunal." [15]

The indwelling of Christ's Spirit means not only moral discernment, but moral power. Paul's count against the Law is that it was impotent through the flesh. Against this impotence Paul sets the ethical competence of the Spirit. "I can do anything in Him who makes me strong," he exclaims. For his friends in Asia he prays "that God may grant you, according to the wealth of His splendour, to be made strong with power through His Spirit in the inner man, that Christ may dwell in your hearts through your trust in Him." [16] This is the antithesis of the dismal picture presented in the seventh chapter of the Epistle to the Romans, and it comes, just as evidently as that, out of experience. Indeed, we may say that the thing above all which distinguished the early Christian community from its environment was the moral competence of its members. In order to maintain this we need not idealize unduly the early Christians. There were sins and scandals at Corinth and Ephesus, but it is impossible to miss the note of genuine power of renewal and recuperation—the power of the simple person progressively to approximate to his moral ideals in spite of failures. The very fact that the term "Spirit" is used points to a sense of something essentially "supernatural" in such ethical attainment. For the primitive Christians the Spirit was manifested in what they regarded as miraculous. Paul does not whittle away the miraculous sense when he transfers it to the moral sphere. He concentrates attention on the moral miracle as something more wonderful far than any "speaking with tongues." So fully convinced is he of the new and miraculous nature of this moral power that he can regard the Christian as a "new creation." This is not the old person at all: it is a "new man," "created in Christ Jesus for good deeds." [17]

The result of all this is that the Christian is a free man. It is here to be observed that the term "freedom" is ambiguous in common usage. It is sometimes used to imply that a man can do just as he likes, undetermined by any external force. To this the determinist replies that as a matter of fact this freedom is so limited by the laws which condition man's empirical existence as to be illusory. The rejoinder from the advocates of free will is that no external force can determine a man's moral conduct (and with mere automatism we are not concerned), unless it is presented in consciousness, and that in being so presented it becomes a desire, or a temptation, or a motive. In suffering himself to be determined by these the man is not submitting to external control, but to something which he has already made a part of himself for good or ill. When, however, we have said that, we are faced with a further problem. Not all that is desired is desirable, and in being moved by my immediate desire I may be balking myself of that ultimate satisfaction which is the real object of all effort. If that is so, then to "do as I like" may well be no freedom at all. There is a law of our being which forbids satisfaction to be found along that line, as it is written, "He gave them their desire, and sent leanness into their souls." He, then, whose action is governed by mere desire is not free to attain the satisfac-

tion which alone gives meaning to that desire. There
is no breaking through this law of our being. Every
attempt to do so proves itself in experience to be
futile. Hence we are in a more hopeless state of
bondage than that which materialistic determinism
holds; for the tyrant is established within our own
consciousness. One way, and one way only, out of
this bondage remains. If we can discover how to
make our own immediate desire, and the act of will
springing out of it, accord with the supreme law of
our being, then to "do as we like" will no longer be
to run our heads against the stone wall of necessity
which shuts us out from the heaven of satisfaction.
For we shall only "like" doing what we "ought." This
introduces a new sense of the word "freedom." It
does not now mean freedom from restraint to follow
our desires, but freedom from the tyranny of futile
desires to follow what is really good.

This is Paul's meaning. The state of slavery described in the seventh chapter of the Epistle to the
Romans is a slavery to wrong desires; not merely to
"flesh" in the abstract, as implying our material nature
and environment, but to the "mind of the flesh"—the
lower nature and environment made a part of one's
conscious self. The slavery is the more intense because there is the Reason or Conscience recognizing
the ideal of true satisfaction, and chafing more and
more at its impotence to resist. What the Law could
not do, God has done by the gift of the Spirit of
Christ: He has given the victory to the higher self.
"Where the Spirit of the Lord is, there is liberty."
"The Law of the Spirit—the law of a life in communion with Christ Jesus—has made me free from the law
of sin and death." Whereas life was a hopeless struggle, in which the higher self was handicapped against
a foe that had all the advantage, it now becomes a
struggle in which the handicap is removed, and victory already secured in principle, because God has

come into the life. The Law was external; it was a taskmaster set over against the troubled and fettered will of man. The Spirit is within, the mind of the Spirit is the mind of the man himself, and from within works out a growing perfection of life which satisfies the real longing of the soul. In the full sense freedom is still an object of hope; but the liberty already attained makes possible the building up of a Christian morality.

XI

THE DIVINE COMMONWEALTH
DISCOVERED

From Paul's teaching about the Spirit of Christ flows
naturally a thought in which we may find the consummation of his work. Where many individuals
share an experience so intimate as the "partnership of
the Son of God" there must be a very intimate unity
among them. Moved and governed by the same
Spirit, they are one at the deepest levels of life. The
new life in Christ, while it rests upon a most intensely individual experience, is yet a life in which no
man is a mere individual. He is a member of Christ's
Body. We may recall that for Paul "body" meant a
real organic identity such as that which makes a man
a single self-identical individual through all the
changes of the years. Wherever Christ's Spirit is at
work, there is His body; and He has only one body.
Thus the immense varieties of spiritual activity are
only aspects of the one life, analogous to the functions of various organs in a living body—hand, eye,
ear. Each is necessary to all, and each gets its significance only from its place in the whole. There is one
Spirit. and therefore through the whole area of the

human race there can only be one body. Here the
evolution of monotheism reaches its necessary conclusion. "There are varieties of gifts, but the same Spirit;
and there are varieties of services, but the same Lord;
and there are varieties of activities, but the same
God, who is the source of all activity in us all." "There
is one body and one Spirit . . . one God and Father
of all, who is above all, and through all, and in all." [1]
This drawing of the last inference from the development of a great religious principle is a signal contribution of Paul to social philosophy. The Stoics had
already reached a doctrine of the unity of man. Here,
as in other points, Paul stands right in the midst of
wide streams of thought. But it may be observed that
the Stoic doctrine was worked out wholly within a system of naturalistic Pantheism, and suffered from the
limitations which such a philosophy involves. Paul's
Christian doctrine of the unity of man has its center
in a moral self-revelation of the one God, knitting
together all men who will accept a moral and personal relation to Him.

So much for the theory of the matter. But important as was Paul's theoretical contribution, it was not
a mere matter of theory. It represents the actual experience of the early days of Christianity. When a
number of individuals with varying and even clashing
interests have been caught by a revolutionary force
which has made some one new interest mean more
to each than any of his previous interests, then a new
unity is inevitably created. This is what actually
happened to the early Christians. The fact of Christ
and His dealing with them became more important
to each than any other fact of his experience. The
separate interests of master and slave, man and
woman, Jew and Gentile, man of culture and barbarian, faded into nothing before the absorbing fact
which made each of these a Christian. Christ lived
in each. and therefore the life of all was one.[2] One of

Paul's great words is that which is variously translated "communion" or "fellowship." The Greek word is *koinonia,* which was originally a commercial term implying co-partnership or common possession. Thus in the Gospels the sons of Zebedee and of John are said to have been *koinonoi,* or partners, in a kind of joint-stock company owning fishing-boats. This word seemed to the early Christians the most appropriate term to describe their relations one to another. They were co-partners in a great estate—the splendid spiritual "heritage" in which they were "joint-heirs with Christ." The ground of their corporate life was what they called "partnership of the Spirit"—a joint-ownership in all that was most real and vital to them all. Our liturgical phrase "the communion of the Holy Ghost" curiously obscures the vividness of the original words, as Paul passed them down to us.[3]

Here, then, as Paul saw with a sudden clearness of vision, was in actual being that holy commonwealth of God for which the ages waited. Here was a community created not by geographical accident or by natural heredity, not based on conquest, or wealth, or government, but coming into existence by the spontaneous outburst of a common life in a multitude of persons. The free, joyous experience of the sons of God had created a family of God, inseparably one in Him: "one person in Christ Jesus."

This is not to say that all distinctions between men are blurred in a dull uniformity. For the irrelevant distinctions of class, race, and nationality, which set men in hostility, are substituted those differentiations of function which bind men together in a co-operative commonwealth. Paul had much ado to induce his Greek converts, born individualists as they were, to give full play to this unity in difference. The Corinthians made even the varied endowments of the Christian life matters of competition and rivalry. They had no criterion of worth, but judged a man's

gifts solely by their "rarity value." Paul bade them
apply a new test; the up-building of the body. We
have seen how Paul criticized the "revival" phenomena of the early period. This was the test by which he
judged them. "Speaking with tongues" was of small
value: it profited no one but the individual. "Prophecy" was of greater value: it benefited the community. The endowment of the Christian was an endowment for service; the variety of endowments pointed
to an organism with a variety of functions. Since the
endowments came from the Lord the Spirit, it was He
alone who could give meaning and reality 'ɔ the
whole. It was as His Body that the whole community
functioned.[4] Pursuing this line of thought, Paul was
led to see that the gifts and endowments which are of
vital importance are the moral virtues, and above all,
love, which is "the perfect link." This divine love or
charity is the subject of Paul's famous lyrical passage
in the thirteenth chapter of his First Epistle to the
Corinthians. It is the highest and most comprehensive
gift of the Spirit. "The love of God is shed abroad in
our hearts by the Holy Spirit given to us." [5]

Thus the highest category of Christian ethics is de-
duced by Paul directly from the experience of the indwelling Spirit of Christ, and we may find in the fact a
confirmation of the reality of his claim to guidance by
Christ's Spirit; for the central thing in the teaching of
Jesus is His enthronement of love to God and man as
the supreme and sufficient law of human conduct.
Paul is moving in different regions of thought, yet
emerges at the same point; and when he claims that
in spite of the manifest differences of the route his
guide to the goal has been Christ Himself, we must
allow that his claim has reason. Love, then, is the
sum-total of moral obligation: "Be under no obligation to anyone except the obligation of love. For love
is the fulfilment of law." It is a creative principle of
society, the actual force which builds and keeps in be-

ing the mystical body of emancipated humanity, the "Israel of God." It is the groundwork of the new "Law of Christ" or "Law of the Spirit." [6]

Here we find the necessary and sufficient correction to the individualism of Paul's ethic of the Spirit. The sense of a supernatural intuition of God and His will, independent of tradition or the mediation of any authority, is apt, if taken alone, to strengthen individual self-reliance to a morbid degree. It "puffs up," says Paul. But if the revealing spirit is the Spirit of Christ, then also it is the Spirit of love, and "while knowledge puffs up, love builds up"; builds up, not the character of the individual being—we do less than justice to Paul if we so interpret him—but builds up the commonwealth of God into an ordered and organic whole. [7]

As the initiation of the Christian life, that "immersion in one Spirit" in which the believer died and rose again with Christ, had its proper symbol in the rite of baptism, so also the fellowship of the Body of Christ had its symbol in the "Lord's Supper." From the beginning the Christian communities had their common meal, the "breaking of bread," and although we have not any explicit account of the meaning which before Paul's time was attached to the custom, yet the primitive record states that the Lord at His last meal with His disciples broke bread, saying "This is My body"; and His followers can hardly have continued to break the bread without some recollection of His words, or without attaching some special meaning to them. For Paul, at any rate, the breaking of the bread which Christ had called His body was "a sharing in the Body of Christ": "because there is one loaf, we, who are many, are one body, for we all share in the one loaf." [8] In order to understand what Paul meant to say by that, we must remember how absolutely seriously he took the thought that the life of the Christian is the life of Christ. As the "soul," or

principle of life (*psyché*) animates the body of flesh,
so the Spirit (of Christ) animates the community.
When bread is eaten, the virtue of it passes into all
the members of the body. So in receiving Christ, the
Body, which is the community, nourishes all its several members and they are inseparably one in the
sharing of the common life.

There is behind this a deep mystical thought resem-
bling that of the higher mystery cults of the Greeks,
in which the sacred food of the God was eaten, and
the worshipper became one with Him. But Paul will
not let the matter rest at that quasi-magical level at
which the mere consumption of consecrated elements
by itself sufficed to work some mystic change. The
reality underlying the meal is Christ's impartation of
Himself in His Spirit to His people. But that Spirit is
love. If love be not an actual and effectual force in
the gathering of believers, then the form is utterly
empty and has no value. When at Corinth the Christians came together in a selfish and individualist spirit,
they were not eating the Lord's Supper, but their
own. There were quarrels and rivalries. The rich
feasted in luxury; the poor looked on and hungered,
and the rich despised them. Under these conditions,
says Paul, it was quite impossible to eat a true "Supper of the Lord." It was useless to take the bread and
say, "This is the Lord's Body," when you did not
"discern the Body"—the unity which His Spirit
creates among those who have the love of God shed
abroad in their hearts. For the Supper was also a
solemn memorial of the dying of Christ, and of all
that the dying meant. It reminded the partakers that
they were crucified with Christ—dead to the evil passions of the unsanctified heart, its selfishness and
greed. The cup of wine was a participation in Christ's
sacrifice—the blood of the new covenant. The Supper
is therefore more than an ordinary community-meal,
and more also than the consuming of sacred food

which brings magical potency with it: it is the current renewal of a union with Christ both in His death and in His risen life, and so a repeated, "crucifixion of the flesh with the affections and lusts," and a repeated constitution of Christ's Body in the renewal of mutual love through His Spirit.

In this Body of Christ Paul sees "the *ecclesia* of God." *Ecclesia* is a Greek word with a splendid history. It was used in the old free commonwealths of Greece for the general assembly of all free citizens, by which their common life was governed. When political liberty went, the name still survived in the restricted municipal self-government which the Roman State allowed. It was taken over by the brotherhoods and guilds which in some measure superseded the old political associations. Among the Jews who spoke Greek this word seemed the appropriate one to describe the commonwealth of Israel as ruled by God—the historical Theocracy. Our translation of it is "Church." That word, however, has undergone such transformations of meaning that it is often doubtful in what sense it is being used. Perhaps for *ecclesia* we may use the word, simpler, more general, and certainly nearest to its original meaning—"Commonwealth." We have spoken throughout of the Divine Commonwealth. That phrase represents Paul's "*ecclesia* of God." [9] It is a community of loving persons, who bear one another's burdens, who seek to build up one another in love, who "have the same thoughts in relation to one another that they have in their communion with Christ." [10] It is all this because it is the living embodiment of Christ's own Spirit. This is a high and mystical doctrine, but a doctrine which has no meaning apart from loving fellowship in real life. A company of people who celebrate a solemn sacrament of Christ's Body and Blood, and all the time are moved by selfish passions—rivalry, competition, mutual contempt—is not for Paul a Church or Divine Commonwealth at all, no matter how lofty their faith or how deep their mystical experience; for all these things may "puff up"; love alone "builds up."

In the very act, therefore, of attaining its liberty to exist, the Divine Commonwealth has transcended the great divisions of men. In principle it has transcended them all, and by seriously living out that which its association means, it is on the way to comprehending the whole race. Short of that its development can never stop. This is the revealing of the sons of God for which the whole creation is waiting.

XII

THE LIFE OF THE DIVINE COMMONWEALTH

Paul, as a Pharisee, was supremely concerned with conduct, for in Judaism not orthodoxy but correctness of conduct was the test of a religious man. The standard of conduct was external and confused trivialities of ritual with the "weightier matters of the Law." But conduct was the all-important thing. When Paul became a Christian he did not lose his interest in practical religion. In his greatest theological epistle the high argument reaches a climax when with *"therefore, my brothers, I urge you . . ."* he turns to show how the sum and substance of the whole is moral holiness in practical life.[1]

In the ethical teaching he gives we must think of him as a missionary seeking to train a Christian community in the midst of a heathen society. He could not, and would not, do so by any attempt to impose a rigid code governing all behaviour. His aim was to see "Christ formed in them." He wished to see them enter into that self-determining life of fellowship with Christ which means emancipation of the spirit of man. That life of fellowship with Christ means

also membership of a body. From these two principles—the Spirit of Christ in the individual, the Spirit
of Christ creating the body—all morality must spring
by the pure and free submission of individuals to the
leading of that Spirit. All that Paul could do was to
set forth by way of example the kind of way in which
such leading tended for people situated as his correspondents were situated in the Roman world. In its
particulars his ethical teaching embodies a good deal
of the new morality which contemporary Stoicism
was proclaiming, as well as of the humaner Jewish
morals of the tradition of Jesus ben Sirach and the
"Wisdom" literature. The wise moral teacher will express the ideals he wishes to promulgate as far as possible in terms already appreciated by his hearers.
But the unity of the whole depends upon an inform-
ing spirit. It is the character of Christ which makes it
a whole. "I urge you by virtue of the meekness and
sweet-reasonableness of Christ"; "Bear one another's
burdens, and so fulfil the law of Christ"; "whatever
you do, in act or word, do everything in the name of
the Lord Jesus": when Paul uses such language it is
more than a form of words.[2] It represents a settled
and reasonable conviction, first that where there is
knowledge of good among men it is the work of
Christ the life-giving Spirit, and secondly that now
that Christ has lived the human life we have a clear
line of definition, a test for all our moral intuitions. In
the whole of Paul's moral teachings a single and self-
consistent ideal is implied, and that ideal is the character of Jesus Christ. If we take as the vital center of
Pauline ethics the poem of love in the thirteenth
chapter of the First Epistle to the Corinthians, we
shall not be wrong in recognizing in it a portrait for
which Christ Himself has sat. What Paul was trying to
do was to show how a man would live if Christ were
living in him, at Corinth, at Ephesus, at Rome, in the
reign of Nero.

There were certain things which he would avoid as a matter of course: they were forbidden by the best conscience of heathendom. Indeed, the catalogues of vices which Paul gives correspond fairly closely with those of contemporary moralists. He generally groups them broadly into two classes: sins of the flesh, of lust and appetite, and anti-social vices, especially the commercial vices, summed up as "greed" or "over-reaching" *pleonexia*.[3] I say "as a matter of course": and such it was for Paul, but not for his converts. We are startled to find gross unchastity at Corinth, theft at Ephesus, drunkenness at both. The fact is that Paul had addressed himself to an audacious enterprise in calling into the Church the very riff-raff of society. If we ask how this man—brought up in a narrowly pietistic Puritan sect—reached such faith in human nature, we remember that he was a follower of the Friend of publicans and sinners and find the answer there. But that these evil things must go he never doubted; and he assailed them in a steady confidence that Christ had given the victory.

Over against these vices Paul does not set any merely negative asceticism. He does not correct unchastity by demanding monkish celibacy, or avarice by insisting on Franciscan poverty, or drunkenness by erecting total abstinence into a law. In the Epistle to the Colossians he blazes out against the asceticism of certain circles as a denial of the supremacy of Christ over all creation and of the freedom of the Christian man. "All things are yours; and you are Christ's, and Christ is God's," is his broad principle.[4] His doctrine of "mortification"[5] is something far removed from that of subsequent Catholicism: it is not the ascetic discipline which is a kind of reversed self-pampering, but the complete dissociation of oneself from all selfish, self-regarding, self-protecting impulses, and the readiness to accept the consequences of that dissociation in loss, contumely, persecution

or hardship to body or soul. In his First Epistle to the
Corinthians there is a passage which affords an interesting study in the light of this.[6] Its conclusion is
perhaps the most "ascetic" passage in Paul: and the
context merits examination. The point at issue is
Paul's refusal to take money for his services. It was
the custom of wandering preachers of the Cynic,
Stoic, and other sects to receive gifts from their hearers. Jesus Christ had sanctioned the expectation of
hospitality on the part of His followers: and Peter at
least seems to have interpreted this as including main-
tenance for his wife. "All quite right and proper," says
Paul; "but I personally should find it a hindrance. I
prefer to bear my own burden. Similarly I am prepared to yield even the liberty which I claim for every
Christian; I am ready to put myself beside weak-
minded persons and accept restrictions which they
consider necessary. I am prepared to give up anything which interferes with the success of my mission, as the athlete surrenders what would incapaci-
tate him for running, and if 'brother ass, the body' [7]
protests—so much the worse for brother ass! But I
am bringing brother ass to heel: he shall not balk me
in the end." If that is asceticism, then Paul is an
ascetic. He has got work to do which must be done,
and that work is his consuming passion. As the boxer
trains hard and the racer runs light, so he will drop
what hinders him from pressing towards the mark.
That is different from the timid "touch not, taste not,
handle not," of the Colossian ascetics, and from the
later ecclesiastical prohibitions and restraints.

On one point, however, Paul seems untrue to himself. A little later, we learn there were ascetics at
Ephesus who taught abstention from marriage, and
probably claimed Paul's sanction.[8] If so, he had only
himself to blame.[9] For himself he deemed the re-
nunciation of family life necessary for his mission,
though he had as much *right* to marry as Peter,

James, and the rest. So far, so good: but when he wished others, not engaged in mission work, to follow his example, and suggested that marriage was a *pis aller,* he was on less safe ground. There is much to be said for Sir William Ramsay's view that Paul was concerned in the first instance to maintain his right to be a bachelor if his work demanded it. To the normal Jew there was something eccentric, if not worse, about celibacy, and among the Greeks the man who did not marry was "asking for" scandal. Paul set out to claim that a full, pure, and honourable life could be lived, and by some must be lived, outside marriage. But he was carried away, as so many people are, into proving too much. We shall do best to hold him fast, in this matter and on the whole question of the relations of the sexes, to his more humane and truly Christian teaching that while in Christ there is neither male nor female, the pure love of man and wife is a sacrament of the divine love of Christ, and the marriage relation which it consecrates is indissoluble.[10]

The frontal attack on evil living is not by way of ascetic regulations, but by a steady appeal to the new life in Christ. Thus, he writes to the Christians of Salonica:[11]

God called us, not for an impure life, but into a life of holiness. And so any one who neglects (this calling) neglects not man but God who gives to us His Holy Spirit. About love for the brotherhood, again, there is no need for me to write to you, for you yourselves are taught by God to love one another; and indeed you act accordingly towards all the brothers in all Macedonia. But I beg you, my brothers, to do still better (in this direction), and to take pains to lead a quiet life, to mind your own business, and to work with your own hands, as I told you; so that your conduct may be respectable in the eyes of outsiders, and that there may be no destitution among you.

There is sound sense in these injunctions to an excitable and unsteady people. Here and everywhere Paul impresses us with his readiness to trust the Christian impulse and illumination in his very fallible converts. Again and again he echoes the appeal of Jesus, "Why do ye not even of yourselves judge that which is right?" [12] And from the same root grows as of necessity the whole new life. "The fruit of the Spirit is love, joy, peace, patience, kindness, goodness, loyalty, self-control." [13]

But further, the Spirit is a corporate possession and not a merely individual. There is a "partnership of the Spirit." That fact given full play creates from a new center the whole ethical life. In the twelfth chapter of the Epistle to the Romans we see the Christian ethic growing out of the thought of the claim of the body upon each of its members. The Epistle to the Ephesians supplies the fullest working out of this.[14] It is interesting to survey this broad sketch of Christian community-life and observe how at each stage there is an appeal to the central principles of life "in Christ." Speak the truth—for we are members one of another. Let the thief stop thieving, let him work hard—in order that he may have something to bring into the common store. Mutual regard must take the place of envy, hatred, malice, and all uncharitableness, "as Christ loved you and sacrificed Himself for you." Injuries must be blotted out by forgiveness "as God in Christ forgave you." "The Kingdom of Christ and God" rules out alike unchastity and avarice or the idolatry of Mammon. Mutual subjection is the rule. This begins in the family, where the relation of husband and wife is a "mystery" or sacrament of the relation of Christ and His Church. Parents and children have mutual duties and responsibilities "in the Lord." Slaves must give obedience "as Christ's slaves doing the will of God," and masters must "do just the same" to the slaves, because masters too are slaves of Christ.

What we need to observe here is the conception of mutual responsibility founded on an identical relation to Christ. Paul has taken over the framework of the household as known to Greek, Roman, and Jewish law: the housefather as supreme lord and disposer of his wife, his children and his slaves. But in doing so he has introduced a revolutionary principle which was bound to transform the whole conception. In regard to slavery Christianity brought reinforcements to Stoicism in the protest it was making against that deeprooted institution. Its attack was made from a different side. Stoicism started in the main from the natural unity and equality of men, and showed that slavery as an institution was illogical. Christianity started from the slave himself as a son of God, and so a "brother for whom Christ died." It did not at the outset say that the institution was indefensible. It introduced a new attitude to the slave as a man. This new attitude is well illustrated from the letter which Paul wrote to his friend Philemon of Colossæ. He had lost a slave, Onesimus, who had run away with money belonging to his master. By some means Paul came in touch with the slave, and brought him to a better mind. He induced him to return to his master, with a letter from Paul. In this letter he wrote: "I beg you for my son Onesimus, born to me in my prison. A 'good-for-nothing' he was once, but now he is good for much, both to me and to you. I have sent him back to you as though I sent you my own heart. . . . It may be that he was separated from you for a time for this reason, that you might get him back no longer as a slave, but something better than a slave, a dear brother—dear certainly to me, and surely dearer far to you, both by natural relations and in (communion with) the Lord." There is here a transforming power which goes deeper even than the splendid humanism of the Stoics. We may recall that even Epictetus, one of the noblest of them, could dissuade a man from punishing a slave in the words "It is better for your slave to be bad than for you to make yourself unhappy." [15]

Passing beyond the household we have the growing community. In pre-Roman times the Greek city-state had formed a real community, where the individual was conscious of having his part in the "general will." The system had collapsed, and for all the elaborate organization of the Empire with its local and central government there was no real community wherein a man could find that whole-hearted fellowship with others in common concerns which is necessary to a full life. A similar problem faces us today, and provokes the various schemes of Syndicalism and the "Soviet" idea. The result in the Roman Empire was the formation of religious and semi-religious guilds, of which the central government was perpetually jealous, which it tried time and time again to cripple but never dared utterly to destroy. The Christian Church was the biggest attempt to create a real community within the amorphous society of the Roman world. In large measure it succeeded, because it based itself upon a real experience of fellowship founded upon a free and personal relation to a "Lord" whose character was definite and known—a personal relation which was one of "faith" or complete confidence. We see the conception of mutual responsibility working itself out in the community.[16]

We urge you, brothers, give good advice to the disorderly, console the timorous, hold the weak by the hand, and be patient with everybody.

Each member must have something worth bringing into the common store.[17]

For just as we have many organs in one body, and these organs have not all the same function, so we, many as we are, constitute one body in (communion with) Christ, while we are individually organs of one another. And so, since we have different gifts, corresponding to God's graciousness shown to us, if the gift be inspired preaching, let us preach up to the full measure of our conviction; if it be administration, (let us throw ourselves) into administration; if it be teaching, into teaching; if it be the encouragement of others, into encouragement; a man who gives should do it open-heartedly, one who takes the lead, with energy, one who does a kindness, with cheerfulness.

And this applies to material as well as spiritual things. The principle is enunciated by Paul quite incidentally. During the central portion of his career as a missionary he set on foot a great scheme by which he hoped to promote that unity between Jewish and Gentile Christians which was one of his dearest aims. The Christian community in Judæa was in great poverty, from various causes, including famine and probably persecution. Paul projected an extensive Relief Fund, to which all his communities of converts from paganism should contribute as a mark of brotherly love, and also as some acknowledgment of the real debt which they owed to the first promulgators of the Christian faith. The latter point Paul puts to the Romans in these terms:[18]

Macedonia and Achaia have decided to make a "sharing-out" (*koinonia*) for the poor among the Holy Community at Jerusalem. They decided—and indeed it was their bare duty; for if the pagans shared in (the verb is *koinonein*) their spiritual possessions, it is only fair that they should help the Jews with their material possessions.

It is almost impossible to reproduce in English the play upon the world *koinonia* which makes it clear that the "partnership" of Christians is a partnership in material goods as well as in spiritual. Here is a basis for a far-reaching Christian communism. Hence the motive Paul suggests for work, which is capable of a wider and more fruitful application. Paul, we may observe, brought into Greek society, with its affected contempt for the "vulgarity" of all handiwork, the healthier Jewish tradition of respect for the craftsman. But observe the motive: "A man should labour with his hands, that he may have something to give to him who has need." [19] In other words, Work not for gain, but to enrich the community. Mr. Bernard Shaw's dictum, "Do your work for love and let the other people lodge and feed and clothe you for love," is an equally good, if rough, expression for the teaching of Paul as it is for that of Jesus.[20]

The interaction of the two principles of individual autonomy and mutual responsibility is well illustrated by Paul's dealing with some questions of casuistry which arose out of the clash of different races and cultures in the Church. At Corinth a difficulty arose about the eating of food which had received a pagan consecration. The difficulty could not be avoided. If you belonged to any sort of social club or trade guild, you could not go to the members' dinner without having food over which a pagan "grace before meat" had been said. If you dined out with friends, the same thing might happen. And anyhow, you never knew but that the meat you bought at the butcher's had done duty in some sacrifice. In the Forum of Pompeii, indeed, the chapel of the Divine Emperor stands between the place of slaughter and the butcher's shop. The close connexion of sacrifice with the sale of meat is clear. Here was a strange dilemma for a person who believed that such a consecration brought demonic influence into the food. The Jew, then as now, would not touch such "unclean" meat. The conscience of the primitive Church was equally tender about it.[21] No wonder, then, that many at Corinth felt in the same way. But others, inspired by Paul's teaching, said: "No, an idol is nothing in the world; there is nothing in it." And they freely and openly ate the consecrated food, to the great scandal of the "weak-minded brother." "Everything is lawful" was their watchword. Had not Christ "made all meats clean"? Paul retorts: "Everything may be lawful; but not everything builds up (the community). It is not everyone who has this robust faith, and if a weaker-minded brother follows your lead and eats, in the ineradicable belief that he is incurring defilement, you have injured his conscience, and you are responsible for him." [22] A similar difficulty arose at Rome over Sabbath-keeping and vegetarianism, and Paul deals with it similarly: All days are alike; all foods are legitimate; but if your faith does not really rise to that height, then you must not go a step further than your conscience allows. "That which does not spring out of conviction is sin." And if there is a "brother" who has scruples you must not indulge your liking till you have won him to your way of thinking. "Do not ruin with your eating the brother for whom Christ died." [23]

What we have here to note is the immense value attached to the individual conscience. No community can be "built up," Paul says, except upon a tender and sincere regard for the conscience of its members, even though the conscience be mistaken or over-scrupulous. On the other hand, the robust conscience is bound to criticize with a candid eye the whole field of obligation and duty, unhampered by *tabus* or superstitious fears; moved only by the consciousness of a relation to Christ within the conscience which must never be desecrated, and by a perpetual sense of responsibility towards others; "for no one lives to himself and no one of us dies to himself."

Finally, the growing Christian community aims at comprehending all humanity. Meanwhile, its task unfinished, it has relations to "the outsiders." First, the Christian has a duty to the conscience of his pagan

neighbours. He is bound to respect their moral standards to the utmost of his power. "Think out conduct
which shall be honourable in the judgment of all
men." [24] But further, the obligation to a general
beneficence which love entails is not limited by the
bounds of the Christian community: "as we have
opportunity let us do good to *all,* especially to members of the family of faith." "Never return evil for
evil, but always pursue what is good both towards
one another and towards all." "I am debtor," Paul
said, "to Greeks and barbarians." That debt he sums
up in the same epistle as "to love one another." [25] That
love will inspire the most scrupulous discharge of all
social duties. The emperor and his government come
within the scope of this general obligation, the more
so because, however imperfectly, the empire does
seek to embody something of that natural law of recompense which can only be transcended as men enter into the higher life of love and liberty in Christ.[26]
But love will lead to something more positive than
the mere discharge of duties. For all the measure of
good that there is in paganism, there is also a power
of evil, which is exerted by way of opposition to the
Christian community. This is to be met always, not
merely with non-resistance, but with an overplus of
good. "If possible, keep the peace with all, so far as
the decision lies with you. Do not seek revenge, dear
friends, but let the Nemesis of sin have its course.
. . . Do not be conquered by evil, but conquer evil
with good." [27] This is surely an admirable summary
and application of the teachings on non-resistance in
the Sermon on the Mount. The outcome of it all is that
the principle of reciprocity—"an eye for an eye, and
a tooth for a tooth"—which in the old religion defined
the nature of the divine dealing and therefore of
moral obligation as between men, is superseded by
the new positive and creative principle of love. Because love is the only principle upon which God deals

with us, it is the only foundation of human morality.

In all this it is implied that society as constructed on a pagan basis must pass away. The future lies with the new community created by the Spirit of Christ. The future of mankind is entrusted to this community, and its history must be the growth and consolidation of this community. Its members are as "luminaries in the world, holding out the word of truth." [28] They are "elect" for a purpose—the purpose of bringing into God's way and into the fellowship of His Son the whole race of mankind without distinction. In looking forward, therefore, Paul can concentrate attention upon the fortunes of Christ's Body. In it he sees the promise of a true commonwealth of man. Already within the borders of the Christian Society the great distinctions of race, sex, culture, status, are transcended, and the autonomous company of believers at Ephesus or Rome is a real nucleus of the universal commonwealth. He sees this commonwealth growing up, built on the foundation of apostles and prophets —lives of men illuminated, inspired, and sanctified— with Christ for corner-stone; a temple inhabited by the Spirit of God. Or again, he sees it as a living organism—Christ the Head, every joint playing its part in consolidating the living structure, till it grows into perfect humanity. Then as his vision broadens he sees this "full-grown man" made the means of the redemption of the universe which waits in hope for the revelation of the sons of God. For God who "was in Christ reconciling the world to Himself" has purposed in the end "to sum up in Christ all things in heaven and earth." [29] That vision of a world made one and free was the inspiration of the apostle's life-work, and it is the word of hope he passes on to a distracted race.

APPENDIX

A LETTER FROM PAUL THE MISSIONARY TO THE SOCIETY
OF CHRISTIANS IN ROME

The following abridged paraphrase of the Epistle to
the Romans aims at presenting in a plain way the
continuous sequence of the argument, while suggesting the free epistolary form of the original[1]:

My Dear Fellow-Christians of Rome,
   Wherever I go I hear of your faith, and I thank
God for it. It is a part of my daily prayers that I may
be permitted to visit you. I believe such a visit would
do you good, and I am sure it would do me good. In
fact, I have tried again and again to get to Rome,
but hitherto something has always turned up to prevent me. I shall not feel that my work as missionary
to the Gentiles is complete until I have preached in
Rome. My mission is a universal one, knowing no
bounds of race or culture—naturally, since my message is a universal one. It is a message of God's

righteousness, revealed to men on a basis of faith (i. 1-17).

Apart from this, there is nothing to be seen in the world of today but the Nemesis of sin. Take the pagan world: all men have a knowledge of God by natural religion; but the pagan world has deliberately turned its back upon this knowledge, and, for all its boasted philosophy, has degraded religion into idolatry. The natural consequence is a moral perversity horrible to contemplate (i. 18-32).

But you, my Jewish friend, need not dwell with complacency upon the sins of the pagan world. You are guilty yourself. Do not mistake God's patience with His people for indulgence. His judgments are impartial. Knowledge or ignorance of the Law of Moses makes no difference here. The pagans have God's law written in their conscience. If they obey it, well; if not, they stand condemned. And as for you— you call yourself a Jew and pride yourself on the Law. But have you kept all its precepts? You are circumcised and so forth: that goes for nothing; God looks at the inner life of motive and affection. An honest pagan is better than a bad Jew in His sight. I do not mean to say there is no advantage in being a Jew: [of this more presently;] but read your Bible and take to yourself the hard words of the prophets—spoken, remember, not to heathens, but to people who knew the Law, just as you do. No, Jew and pagan, we are in the same case. No one can stand right before God on the basis of what he has actually *done.* Law only serves to bring consciousness of guilt (ii. 1—iii. 20).

But now, Law apart, we have a revelation of God's righteousness [as I was saying (i. 17)]. It comes by faith, the faith of Jesus Christ; and it comes to *every one,* Jew or Gentile, who has faith. We have all sinned, and all of us can be made to stand right with God. That is a free gift to us, due to His graciousness. We are emancipated in Christ Jesus, who is

God's appointed means of dealing with sin—a means operating by the devotion of His life, and by faith on our part. It is thus that God, having passed over sins committed in the old days when He held His hand, demonstrates His righteousness in the world of to-day; i.e. it is thus that He both shows Himself righteous, and makes those stand right before Him who have faith in Jesus Christ. No room for boasting here! No distinction of Jew and Gentile here! (iii. 21-31).

But what about Abraham? you will say. Did not *he* win God's graciousness by what he *did*? Not at all. Read your Bible, and you will find that the promise was given to him *before* he was circumcised; and the Bible expressly says that "he had faith in God, and *that* counted for righteousness." The same principle applies to us all (chap. iv.).

[To return to the point, then.] We stand right with God on the ground of faith, and we are at peace with Him, come what may. God's love floods our whole being—a love shown in the fact that Christ died for us, not because we were good people for whom anyone might die, but actually while we were sinners. He died, not for His friends, but for His enemies. Very well then, if while we were enemies Christ died for us, surely He will save us now that we are friends! If He reconciled us to God by dying for us, surely He will save us by living for us, and in us. There is something to boast about! (v. 1-11).

[Christ died and lives for us all, I say. But, you ask, how can the life and death of one individual have consequences for so many?] You believe that we all suffer for Adam's sin; and if so, why should we not all profit by Christ's righteousness? Of course there is really no comparison between the power of evil to propagate itself and the power of good to win the victory, for *that* is a matter of God's graciousness. However, you see my point: one man sinned—a whole race suffers for it; one Man lived righteously—a whole

race wins life by it. [But what about Law? you say.]
Law only came in by the way, to intensify the consciousness of guilt (v. 12-21).

Now I come to a difficulty. I have heard people say,
"If human sin gives play to God's graciousness, let
us go on sinning to give Him a better chance. Why not
do evil that good may come?" (cf. iii. 8). What non-
sense! To be saved through Christ is to be a dead man
so far as sin is concerned. Think of the symbolism of
Baptism. You go down into the water: that is like
being buried with Christ. You come up out of the
water: that is like rising with Christ from the tomb.
It means, therefore, a new life, a life which comes by
union with the living Christ. You will admit that, once
a man is dead, there is no more claim against him
for any wrong he may have committed. He is like a
slave set free from all claims on the part of his late
master. Think, then, of yourselves as dead. When
you remember the death of Christ, think that you—i.e.
your old bad selves—were crucified with Him. And
when you remember His resurrection, think of yourselves as living with Him, a new life. And above all,
bear in mind that Christ, once risen, does not die
again: and so you, living the new life in Him, need
not die again. I mean, the sin that once dominated
you need not any longer control you; do not let it! You
are freed slaves; do not sell yourselves into slavery
again. Or, if you like to put it so, you are now slaves,
not of Sin, but of Righteousness (a very crude way of
putting it, but I want to help you out). Just as once
you were the property of Sin, and all your faculties
were instruments of wrong, so now you are the property of Righteousness, and every faculty you have
must be an instrument of right. Freed from sin, you
are slaves of God; that is what I mean. The wages
your old master paid was death. Your new Master
makes you a present of life (vi. 1-23).

Or take another illustration. You know that by law

a woman is bound to her husband while he lives; when he is dead she is free; she can marry again if she likes and the law has no claim against her. So you may think of yourselves as having been married to Sin, or to Law. Death has not released you from that marriage bond, [though here the illustration halts], for it is Christ's death that has freed you! Well, anyhow, you are free—free, shall I say, to marry Christ. You had a numerous progeny of evil deeds by your first marriage; you must now produce an offspring of good deeds to Christ. I mean, of course, you must serve God in Christ's spirit (vi. 1—vii. 6).

Now I admit that all this sounds as though I identified law with sin. That is not my meaning. But surely it is clear that the function of law is to bring consciousness of sin; e.g. I should never have known what covetousness was but that the law said "Thou shalt not covet." Such is the perversity of human nature under the dominion of sin that the very prohibition provokes me to covet. There was a time when I knew nothing of Law, and lived my own life. Then Law came, sin awakened in me, and life became death for me. Of course Law is good, but Sin took advantage of it, to my cost. I am only flesh and blood, and flesh and blood is prone to sin. I can see what is good, and desire it, but I cannot practise it; i.e. my reason recognizes the law, and yet I break it through moral perversity. If you like to put it so, there is one law for my reason, the Law of God, and another for my outward conduct, the law of sin and death. It is like a living man chained to a dead body. It is perfect misery. But, thank God, the chain is broken! The law of the Spirit of Life which is in Christ has set me free from the law of sin and death. Christ entered into this human nature of flesh and blood which is under the dominion of Sin. Sin put in its claim to be His master; but Christ won His case; Sin was non-suited, its claim disallowed, and human nature was free. The result is that all the Law stood for of righteousness, holiness, and goodness is fulfilled in those who live by Christ's Spirit. There are two possible forms of human life: there is the life of the lower nature of flesh and blood, of which I have spoken; and there is the life of the spirit. We have Christ's Spirit, and so we can live the life of the spirit. And in the end that Spirit will give new life to the whole human organism (vii. 7—viii. 11).

You see, then, that the flesh-and-blood nature has no claim upon us. We belong to the Spirit. Those who are actuated by that Spirit are sons of God. [I used a while back the expression, "slaves of God"]; but really we are not slaves but sons—sons of heirs of God, like Christ; and when we come into our inheritance, how glorious it will be! (viii. 12-18).

This, however, is still in the future. At the present time the whole universe is in misery, and in its misery it waits for the revelation of God's sons. *Now* all existence seems futile in its transience; and even we still share creation's pangs. But we have hope; and the ground of that hope is the possession of God's Spirit—in a first instalment only, but enough to reckon upon. The fact is that every prayer we utter—yes, even an inarticulate prayer—is the utterance of the Spirit within us. We know that all through God is working with us. His purpose is behind the whole process, and He is on our side. If He gave His Son we can trust Him to give us everything else. He loves us, and nothing in the world or out of it can separate us from His love (viii. 18-39).

[That concludes the present stage of my argument; but before I can proceed to final deductions, I must return to a difficulty already raised (cf. iii. 1-4).] If there is no difference between Jew and Gentile, does all the great past of Israel go for nothing? Do all the promises of Scripture go for nothing? First, let me say how bitterly i regret the exclusion of the Jewish

nation as a body from the new life. I would surrender
all my Christian privileges if I could find a way to
bring them in. But we must recognize facts; and the
first fact is that the nation as a whole never was able
to claim the promises; from the beginning there was
a process of selection. Of the sons of Abraham, Isaac
alone was called; of the sons of Isaac, Jacob only. If
we ask why, there is no answer save that God is bound
by no natural or historical necessity, but intervenes
according to His will. To question that will is as ab-
surd as for the pot to arraign the potter. Then again,
while some members of the Hebrew race have always fallen out, always God has declared His purpose
ultimately to include others, not members of the Hebrew race—and that is just what is now happening.
Now, as I said, I desire nothing more earnestly than
that the whole nation should be saved. But the fact is
that they have deliberately rejected the chance that
was offered them. There is nothing remote or ab-
struse about the Christian message. It is a very simple
thing: acknowledge Jesus as Lord, and believe that
He is alive; that is all. And they cannot say that they
have never heard the message, for Christ has His witnesses everywhere. It looks, then, as if God had rejected His people, as punishment for their obstinacy.
I do not believe it. God's promises cannot go for nothing. In the first place, there has always been, and there
still is, a faithful remnant of the Jewish people. And
in the second place, as for the main body, their present rejection of the message is only a means in God's
Providence for its extension to the Gentiles. The old
olive-tree of Israel stands yet; many of its branches
have been lopped off, and new branches of wild
olive have been engrafted in their place. But God
can engraft the lopped branches on again, if it be His
will; and I believe it is His will, and that in the end
the whole nation will return to Him and inherit the
promises. And if the failure of Israel has meant such

blessing to the world, how much greater blessing will its ultimate salvation bring! God's purpose, as I said at the beginning (cf. i. 16), is universal: He has permitted the whole of humanity, Jew and Gentile alike, to fall under sin, only in order that He may finally have mercy on the whole of humanity, Jew and Gentile alike. How profound and unsearchable are His plans! (chaps. ix.-xi.)

[So now I can take up again my main argument.] If *this* is the way of God's dealing with us, what ought to be our response? Can we do less than offer our entire selves to God as a sacrifice of thanksgiving? How will that work out? In a life lived as by members of one single body. Let each perform his part faithfully. Let love rule all your relations one to another, and to those outside, even to your enemies. Do not regard the Emperor as outside the scope of love, but obey his laws and pay his taxes. Yes, and pay all debts to every one. Love is, in fact, the one comprehensive debt of man to man. If you love your neighbour as yourself, you have fulfilled the whole moral law. But be in earnest about things, for the better day is already dawning (chaps. xii.-xiii.).

I hear you have differences among yourselves about Sabbath-keeping and vegetarianism. Take this matter, then, as an example of what I mean by the application of brotherly love to all conduct. Remember that the Sabbatarian and the anti-Sabbatarian, the vegetarian and the meat-eater, are alike servants of one Master. Give each other credit for the best motives. Do not think of yourself alone; think of your Christian brother, and try to put yourself in his place. If he seems to you a weak-minded, over-scrupulous individual, remember that in any case he is your brother, and that Christ died for him as well as for you, and reverence his conscience. If through your example he should do an act which is harmless in you but sin to him, you have injured his conscience. Is it worth while so to imperil a soul for the sake of your liberty in such external matters? If the other man is weak-minded, and you strong-minded, all the more reason why you should help to bear his burden. Remember, Christ did not please Himself. In a word, Sabbatarian and anti-Sabbatarian, Jew and Gentile, treat one another as Christ has treated you, and God be with you (xiv. 1-xv. 13).

Well, friends, I hardly think you needed this long exhortation from me. You are intelligent Christians, and well able to give one another good advice. Still, I thought I might venture to remind you of a few points; for after all, I do feel a measure of responsibility for you, as missionary to the Gentiles. I have now accomplished my mission as far West as the Adriatic. Now I am going to Jerusalem to hand over the relief fund we have raised in Greece. After that I hope to start work in the West, and I propose to set out for Spain and take Rome on my way. Pray for me, that my errand to Jerusalem may be successful, so that I may be free to visit you (xv. 14-23).

I wish to introduce to you our friend Phœbe. She renders admirable service to our congregation at Cenchraeae. Do all you can for her; she deserves it.

Kind regards to Priscilla and Aquila, Epaenetus, Mary, and all friends in Rome.

(P.S.—Beware of folk who make mischief. Be wise; be gentle; and all good be with you.)

Timothy, Lucius, Jason, Sosipater, and all friends at Corinth send kind regards. (*So do I—Tertius, amanuensis!*)

Glory be to God!

With all good wishes,

Your brother,

PAUL,

Missionary of Jesus Christ

NOTES

FROM JESUS TO PAUL

[1] Forsyth, *Christian Ethic of War*, p. 87: "Did Christ not summon then, the legions it did not suit Him to ask for to avert the Cross?"

[2] Phil. iii. 5-14, Gal. ii. 19-20.

[3] On this matter see J. R. Coates, *The Christ of Revolution*.

A CITIZEN OF NO MEAN CITY

[1] Perhaps the earliest allusion to Jewish money-lenders occurs in a papyrus of the year 41 of our era. The papyrus is a letter to a man in money difficulties, and contains the salutary advice "Beware of the Jews!" See Milligan: *Greek Papyri*, No. 15.

[2] Ac. xxii. 25-28. The fact that Paul learned a trade, that of tent-making, does not necessarily conflict with what is here said of his family's social position.

[3] This assumes that Ἑβραῖος in Phil. iii. 5 has something of the same shade of meaning as in Ac. vi. 1. In any case Paul spoke Aramaic, Ac. xxii. 2, and Aramaic was the language of his inner life: cf. xxvi. 14.

[4] Ac. xxii. 3, Gal. i. 14.

[5] Ac. viii. 1-3, ix. 1-2, Gal. i. 13, I Cor. xv. 9.

[6] Ac. ix. 3-30, xxii. 3-21, xxvi. 4-23, Gal. i. 15-17.

[7] Ac. xv. 1-35, Gal. ii. 1-10.

[8] II Cor. xi. 23-28, I Cor. iv. 9-13, Gal. iv. 13, II Cor. xii. 7-9.

[9] This piece of information is given only in certain MSS. of Ac. xix. 9, but it probably embodies a good tradition.

[10] Ac. xviii. 2-3, 18-20, I Cor. xvi. 19.

[11] I Cor. i. 26, Rom. xvi. 23, Phil. v. 22, Phm. 8-16 (master and slave); the persons who are mentioned as entertaining the local congregation in their house must have been relatively well-to-do: see Rom. xvi. 5, 23, I Cor. xvi. 19, Col. iv. 15, Phm. 2.

[12] The personal traits of the man come out most vividly in the Second Epistle to the Corinthians and in those to the Galatians and Philippians. To read these letters rapidly through, either in the original or in a good modern translation, neglecting for the moment the details of the argument, is the best way to discover the Apostle as a real man.

[13] Ac. xxi.-xxviii. The epistles to the Ephesians, Philippians, Colossians, and Philemon probably belong to the Roman imprisonment.

[14] I cannot remember to whom I owe this allusion to San Paolo fuori le Mura. There seems no reason to reject the tradition that this noble building marks the actual burial-place of the Apostle.

THE HOPE OF THE WORLD

[1] What follows is mainly based on Rom. viii. 18-25.

[2] Quoted from the poem *To Everyman*, by Edith Anne Stewart published in the *Nation*, November 1918.

[3] This is a dominant idea, as I understand it, of Mr. Fearon Halliday's book, *Reconciliation and Reality*.

[4] Rom. i. 19, ii. 14-15.

[5] Rom. xiii. 1-6.

[6] II Thess. ii. 6-7.

[7] Rom. ii. 1-11.

[8] The $\sigma\tau o\iota\chi\epsilon\tilde{\iota}\alpha$ of Gal. iv. 3, 9, Col. ii. 8, 20, are not the material "elements" of which the world is made, but the "phantom intelligences," as Mr. Thomas Hardy might call them, supposed to animate and control the visible universe. Cf. Eph. vi. 12.

[9] Rom. ix., xi. 1-12.

[10] Rom. i. 3-4, Gal. iii. 16-17, 19, iv. 4-5.

[11] Rom. viii. 28-39, Eph. i. 3-14, cf. Gal. i. 15.

[12] κατ' ἐκλογὴν πρόθεσις, Rom. ix. 11. A transposition of the terms would give us "purposive selection," as distinct from merely "natural selection."

[13] Gal. iii. 6-18, Rom. iv.

[14] Rom. ix. 6-29, xi. 4-7, Gal. iii. 7-9.

[15] I Cor. x. 1-10, cf. Rom. iii. 1-20. The word εὐδοκεῖν does not mean approval following upon conduct, but a free self-determination on the part of God; cf. Gal. i. 15, I Cor. i. 21, Col. i. 19, Eph. i. 5, 9, Phil. ii. 13.

[16] Rom. xi. 4, ix. 27-29.

[17] Gal. iii. 23-24, iv. 1-3: note that these statements are made not about any particular individuals, but about the People of God considered as a historical entity.

[18] This is the judgment also of the author of IV Ezra: see iii. 36, "Individual men of note indeed Thou mayst find to have kept Thy precepts; but nations Thou shalt not find" (c. A.D. 100).

[19] I Thess. v. 4-8, II Thess. i. 10, ii. 2, I Cor. i. 8, iii. 13, v. 5, II Cor. i. 14, vi. 2, Rom. xiii. 12-13, Phil. i. 6, 10, ii. 16.

[20] Rom. xvi. 25-26, Col. i. 25-29, and espec. Eph. iii. 1-12.

[21] I Thess. v. 5, I Cor. x. 11. Paul never says in so many words, as does his follower the author to the Hebrews, that Christians possess "the powers of the coming age" (Heb. vi. 5); but something of the kind is implied both in his constant antithesis of Christianity to "this age" (Rom. xii. 2, I Cor. ii. 6-8, II Cor. iv. 4, Gal. i. 4, Eph. ii. 2, etc.), and in his use of eschatological language in the present or perfect tense instead of the future (Rom. i. 17-18, ἀποκαλύπτεται, I Cor. i. 18, II Cor. ii. 15, σωζόμενοι, ἀπολλύμενοι, I Thess. ii. 16 ἔφθασεν ἡ ὀργή etc.).

[22] I Thess. iii. 3, Col. i. 24, Rom. v. 3-5, cf. II Cor. xii. 10, Phil. iii. 10.

[23] I Thess. iv. 13-v, 11, II Thess. ii. 1-10.

[24] Rom. xi. 11-33.

[25] I Cor. xv. 20-28.

[26] Col. i. 17-29, ii. 19, iii. 10-11, Eph. i. 3, ii. 23, cf. Phil. ii. 10-11.

THE QUEST OF THE DIVINE COMMONWEALTH

[1] For passages from Rabbinic tradition setting forth these ideas, see Weber, *System der altsynagogalen palästinischen Theologie* (1880), pp. 14-18. Much of this material is certainly late, but it doubtless represents earlier views. The earliest definite statement I can recall is the saying of R. Akiba, quoted p. 69.

[2] See especially IV Ezra (II Esdras) vi. 55-56: "Thou hast said that for our sakes thou hast created this world. But as for the other nations which are descended from Adam, thou hast said that they are nothing, and that they are like unto spittle, and thou hast likened the abundance ʿ them to a drop on a bucket." This portion of IV Ezra is dated by internal evidence to A.D. 100. The proud self-consciousness of Israel in contrast to the idolatrous Gentiles is finely expressed in Wisdom xv. which offers an instructive comparison with Rom. i-ii.

[3] Mt. xxiii. 15.

[4] Ac. xvii. 26.

[5] Rom. iii. 9-23.

[6] I Cor. xii. 12-14, Eph. ii. 19-22, iv. 4-16; Gal. iii. 26-28, Col. iii. 9-11; Rom. iii. 21-30, Phil. iii. 3-9.

[7] Phil. iii. 20. Πολίτευμα is used specifically of a colony of settlers who in a strange land reproduce the institutions of their μητρόπολις.

[8] Ζωή αἰώνιος (Rom. v. 21, vi. 22-3, Gal. vi. 8, etc.) is properly the life of the αἰών of Messianic power and glory, begun here and now for those who are in "Christ."

[9] Gal. iv. 21-31.

[10] Romain Rolland, *Above the Battle* (Eng. transl. 1916), p. 54.

[11] Stephen was accused of speaking against the Temple and announcing the supersession of the Mosaic Law, Ac. vi. 13-14. It appears that Paul was present at his examination before the Sanhedrin (Ac. viii. 1, xxii. 20) and heard his defence, which, if it is at all faithfully represented by the rather tedious speech in Ac. vii, dwelt upon the temporary and relative character of both Temple and Law.

[12] I Thess. ii. 15-16.

[13] Ac. xv. 5, xxi. 20.
[14] Gal. ii. 1-10, Ac. xv. 7-11.
[15] Gal. ii. 11-14, cf. I Cor. i. 12.
[16] Ac. xxi. 20-30.
[17] Gal. i. 6-9, iii. 1-5, iv. 12-20, v. 1-12, vi. 12-16.
[18] II Cor. xi. 26.

THE ANCIENT WRONG

[1] Gal. v. 15.
[2] Rom. v. 10, Eph. ii. 14.
[3] The antithesis of the two orders of being runs through I Cor. xv. 40-50; cf. Rom. viii. 20-21, II Cor. iv. 16, v. 4.
[4] II. Cor. iv. 16, cf. Rom. vii. 22-23; Rom. ii. 14-15, Col. i. 21, ii. 18, Eph. iv. 18, Phil. iv. 7.
[5] I Cor. xv. 35-54, ii. 12, iii. 3, Gal. v. 17, Rom. viii. 12-13, 23, etc. I believe that the above is a fair description of Paul's "anthropology." But he is not a systematic theologian, and he sometimes uses terms loosely. $\Sigma\tilde{\omega}\mu\alpha$, $\psi\upsilon\chi\dot{\eta}$, $\pi\nu\epsilon\tilde{\upsilon}\mu\alpha$, all appear at times in senses approximating more closely to their popular or vulgar meaning than to the strict Pauline usage.
[6] Rom. viii. 21.
[7] Eph. vi. 12, cf. Gal. iv. 3, 9, Col. ii. 8, 20; the "rulers of this age" who "crucified the Lord of glory" (I Cor. ii. 8) are discarnate intelligences working behind the actions of men. "Angels" are in Paul generally powers hostile to men's salvation, Rom. viii. 38, I Cor. vi. 3, xi. 10, II Cor. xii. 7, Gal. i. 8, Col. ii. 18.
[8] Rom. viii. 20.
[9] Rom. v. 12, 21, vi. 12, 14, 17-23, vii. 8-11, 20, viii. 3.
[10] Rom. v. 12-21, cf. IV Ezra. iii. 21-22, vii. 11-12.
[11] Rom. i. 18-23, 28; cf. passages cited in note 7 above.
[12] Rom. vii. 14, 18, viii. 5-8, Gal. v. 13, 19-21, vi. 8, Col. ii. 13, 18, Eph. ii. 3. It has to be added that in many passages Paul was $\sigma\acute{\alpha}\rho\xi$ in an entirely non-moral sense as standing simply for the physical part of man, e.g. Rom. ix. 3, Gal. iv. 13, Col. i. 22, etc. How easily the one sense passed into the other is shown by a passage like II Cor. x. 2-4.
[13] ('H) $\acute{o}\rho\gamma\dot{\eta}$ ($\tauο\tilde{υ}$) $\theta\epsilon ο\tilde{υ}$ Rom. i. 18, Col. iii. 6, Eph. v. 6;

ἡ ὀργή Rom. iii. 5, v. 9, ix. 22 (possibly with αὐτοῦ), xii. 19, xiii. 5, I Thess. i. 10, ii. 16; ὀργή Rom. ii. 5, 8, iv. 15, ix. 22 (σκεύη ὀργῆς), Eph. ii. 3, I Thess. v. 9.

[14] Rom. ix. 22-23.

[15] Rom. i. 18-32, xi. 8-10.

[16] Rom. ix. 22-24, ii. 4, xi. 32.

[17] Rom. iv. 5, v. 6, vi. 23.

[18] See N. Micklem, *The Open Light* (C.R.S.) ch. iii.

[19] See Mt. vi. 23=Lk. xi. 35, Mt. v. 13=Lk. xiv. 34, cf. Mk. ix. 50, Mk. iii. 29, cf. Mt. xii. 32=Lk. xii. 10, Mk. viii. 35, cf. Mt. x. 39=Lk. xvii. 33, Mt. xxiii. 34-36=Lk. xi. 49-51, Mt. xi. 21-24=Lk. x. 13-15, Lk. xiii. 1-9, etc. The principle running through all such sayings is that of the disastrous consequences of wrong choice in a moral universe: cf. Gal. vi. 7. On the other hand, the characteristic personal activity of God is illustrated in the patient love of the Shepherd and the Father of the Prodigal.

THE TYRANNY OF AN IDEA

[1] Rom. vii. 12, 14.

[2] Mk. ii. 18-20, Mt. vi. 16-18; *Teaching of the Twelve Apostles*, viii. 1.

[3] Deut. xiv. 3-21, xxii. 11-12, Lev. xix, 27, Mk. vii. 3-4.

[4] See especially the saying of Rabbi Akiba (died 135 A.D.) in *Pirke Aboth*, iii. 19: "Beloved are Israel, in that to them was given the precious instrument wherewith the world was created. Greater love was it that it was known to them that there was given to them the precious instrument wherewith the world was created, as it is said, 'For a good doctrine I have given you; forsake not my Torah (Law)'" (translation by Herford). Cf. Psalm cxlvii. 19-20, cxix. 89-96, lxxviii. 1-7, and Rabbinic passages cited by Weber, *op. cit.* pp. 18-25.

[5] "According to the Jewish mind, requital was deeply ingrained in the whole scheme of things. Exceptions there might be, but they were more apparent than real. The most solemn and the most true adage in the world was 'measure for measure.' 'All measures shall pass away, but measure for measure shall never pass away.' The Rabbinic uses of the word *Middah*, Measure, Attribute, Quality,

form a chapter in themselves."—C. G. Montefiore in *Beginnings of Christianity*, ed. Jackson & Lake.

[6] Rom. ii. 28-29.

[7] Gal. iii. 10-11. Several Rabbinic sayings to this effect are quoted in Wetstein's note on Ja. ii. 10, which is an early and unambiguous statement of the principle.

[8] J. A. Hadfield, in *The Spirit* (ed. B. H. Streeter), p. 87.

[9] Rom. viii. 1-2, Phil. iv. 13, Col. i. 24, Gal. ii. 19, vi. 14.

[10] II Cor. iv. 6.

[11] Gal. ii. 19-20.

[12] Rom. v. 6-8, viii. 35-39, II Cor. v. 14-15, 18-19, Col. i. 13-15, Eph. i. 4-7, ii. 4-10, iii. 18-19, v. 1-2.

[13] Gal. iii. 7-22, iv. 21-31, Rom. iv., ix. 7-13.

[14] Rom. ix. 22.

[15] IV Ezra (II Esdras) viii. 31-36, but contrast 37-62; cf. *id.* vii. 47-61, viii. 1-3, ix. 15, 21-22, x. 10; vii. 68, 133. The date is about A.D. 100; but surely it was out of some such position as this that Paul advanced into Christianity.

[16] Rom. ii. 4.

[17] Rom. iii. 25, cf. Ac. xvii. 30.

[18] Rom. x., iv. 3-8, Gal. iii. 11-12, I Cor. x. 4, cf. II Cor. ii. 4-18.

[19] See especially Is. xlv. 8-25, lv. 6-13, lvi. 1, lxi. 10-11, Jer. xxiii. 5-6, xxxiii. 15-16, cf. Dan. ix. 16. The idea is suggested, but scarcely adopted, in IV Ezra viii. 36.

[20] Rom. iii. 26, cf. i. 16-17, with 18 sqq., setting the problem which is solved in iii. 21 sqq.

[21] See Norman Robinson, *Christian Justice*.

[22] Mt. v. 45, xx. 1-16.

[23] Gal. iii. 15, iv. 7.

[24] Rom. v. 20, cf. Gal. iii. 19.

[25] Rom. v. 13-14.

[26] Rom. viii. 3, cf. IV Ezra iii. 20-22.

[27] Ἀκρασία : see *Nicomachean Ethics*, VII. 1-10.

THE SON OF GOD

[1] Rom. viii. 3.

[2] Gal. iv. 4-5.

[3] See especially *The Book of Enoch* (in Charles' *Apocrypha*

and Pseudepigrapha), and IV Ezra (= II Esdras in the English Apocrypha).

I Cor. i. 24, 30. The "Wisdom" idea is best represented by the books of Wisdom and Ecclesiasticus in the English Apocrypha.

[5] Gal. i. 15-16, ii. 19-20, I Cor. ix. 1, xv. 4-8, cf. II Cor. iv. 6, xii. 1-9.

[6] *God the Invisible King*, p. 6, cf. pp. xiii-xiv.

[7] II Cor. iv. 4, Col. i. 13-19, cf. I Cor. viii. 6.

[8] I Cor. xv. 45-49, cf. II Cor. iii. 17.

[9] I Cor. x. 4.

[10] Gal. iv. 4, Rom. i. 3, viii. 3, II Cor. viii. 9, Phil. ii. 6-8.

[11] Eph. iv. 12-15.

[12] Col. i. 19, ii. 9.

[13] Phil. ii. 9-11, Col. i. 18-20, Eph. i. 20-23, I Cor. xv. 23-27, Rom. i. 4, viii. 34, xiv. 9.

[14] I Cor. x. 16-17, xii. 12-27, Rom. xii. 4-5 (cf. also I Cor. vi. 15), Col. i. 18, 24, ii. 19, iii. 15, Eph. i. 23, ii. 5-7, 15-22, iv. 4-16; Rom. viii. 9-11, 17, I Cor. iii. 11, 23, II Cor. iv. 10-11, Col. i. 27, iii. 9-11 (cf. Gal. iii. 28), Eph. iii. 14-19.

[15] I Thess. iv. 13, v. 10, I Cor. xv. 12-28, Eph. i. 10 *et passim*.

[16] II Cor. v. 16-17.

THE DECISIVE BATTLE

[1] Rom. v. 12-21, I Cor. xv. 21-22.

[2] II Cor. v. 21, Rom. viii. 3, vi. 10.

[3] II Cor. v. 14-15, Rom. vi. 5-8.

[4] Rom. xii. 1.

[5] Gen. ix. 4: so Rom. iii. 25, v. 9, I Cor. x. 16, xi. 25, 27, Eph. i. 7, ii. 13, Col. i. 20.

[6] Is. liii. 10-11.

[7] Col. i. 24, II Cor. i. 5-7.

[8] Rom. v. 17-19.

[9] Rom. iii. 23-26.

[10] From this sense of ἱλάσκεσθαι is derived the common usage in pagan inscriptions, ΘΕΟΙΣ ΙΛΑΣΤΗΡΙΟΝ, "a propitiatory offering to the gods"; but it is a mistake to argue directly from this to the Christian use of the noun.

[11] Unless ἱλάσθητί μοι, Lk. xviii. 13, is regarded as such a use; but though passive in form, the verb is virtually

intransitive in meaning—"be propitious," not "be pro-
pitiated."
[12] E.g. Ps. lxiv. 4 (LXX.=lxv. 3, E.T.) Dn. ix. 24 (LXX.).
[13] See Fearon Halliday, *Reconciliation and Reality.*
[14] Gal. iii. 13.
[15] Rom. v. 12, vi. 23, I Cor. xv. 21. This idea is part of Paul's
Jewish heritage. Cf. IV Ezra iii. 7, vii. 118. See also Fearon
Halliday, *op. cit.* pp. 141-146.

EMANCIPATION

[1] I Cor. xiii. 2, cf. Mk. xi. 22-23.
[2] I Thess. i. 8.
[3] Rom. iii. 22, 26, Gal. ii. 16, iii. 22, Eph. iii. 12, Phil. iii. 9
(the genitive is *not* subjective in any case); Col. ii. 5.
Πίστις ἐν Χριστῷ is probably not exactly what we mean
by "faith in Christ": it is rather faith towards God as con-
ditioned by communion with Christ, Col. i. 4, Eph. i. 15.
In Gal. iii. 26 it is doubtful if ἐν Χριστῷ Ἰησοῦ is to be
construed with πίστεως. Outside these three passages the
expression does not occur in Paul.
[4] I Cor. i. 9, x. 13, II Cor. i. 18, I Thess. v. 24.
[5] Eph. ii. 8, Rom. iii. 30, iv. 16, v. 1, ix. 32, Gal. ii. 16, iii. 24,
Eph. iii. 12, 17.
[6] Gal. ii. 19, iii. 1, vi. 14; cf. Ac. xxii. 8-10.
[7] Rom. ii. 15.
[8] Gal. vi. 7, Rom. vi. 23, interpreted by i. 18 sqq.
[9] *Breastplate of St. Patrick.*
[10] Rom. v. 18-19.
[11] *"Much good, some ill he did, so hope all's even,*
And that his soul through mercy's gone to heaven."
So runs the epitaph of Elihu Yale, the founder of Yale
University, on his tombstone in the churchyard of Wrex-
ham, North Wales.
[12] Phil. iii. 9, cf. Rom. vi. 1-11, xiii. 14, Gal. v. 24, Col. iii.
9-11. See also Fearon Halliday, *op. cit.* chs. x.-xii.
[13] Eph. ii. 9, Rom. iii. 27, I Cor. iii. 7 (cf. i. 18-31), iv. 7.
[14] Phil. ii. 13, cf. I Thess. ii. 13, II Cor. iii. 5, I Cor. xii. 6,
Col. i. 29, Eph. i. 19-20, iii. 20-21.
[15] J. A. Hadfield in *The Spirit*, pp. 106, 110.
[16] William James, *Varieties of Religious Experience*, pp. 209-

210. The passages here quoted are taken by James from Starbuck; but the whole of James' discussion of the type of conversion "by self-surrender," in Lecture ix. provides an illuminating comment on Paul.

[17] Rom. v. 1, 9, viii. 30, I Cor. vi. 11.

[18] Phil. iii. 12-14, cf. I Cor. ix. 23-27, Gal. v. 5.

[19] Phil. ii. 12-13. We may observe how this reproduces in new terms what Jesus had said about the Kingdom of God. "It is your Father's good pleasure to give you the Kingdom"; and yet "Seek ye first the Kingdom of God": "The Kingdom of God is like treasure hid in a field, which a man found, and . . . sold all he had and bought that field": "Strait is the gate and narrow the way that leadeth unto life."

[20] Rom. iv. 5.

[21] Ἀπολύτρωσις associated with δικαίωσις Rom. iii. 24, I Cor. i. 30, cf. Eph. i. 7, 14, Col. i. 14. See also Rom. vi. 6-7, 12-23, viii. 2, II Cor. iii. 17, Gal. iv. 1-7, 21-31, v. 1, 23.

[22] See Wordsworth, *Ode to Duty*.

[23] I Cor. vi. 11, i. 30, cf. Rom. vi. 19, I Thess. iv. 3-7, I Cor. iii. 16-17, vi. 19, Eph. ii. 21.

[24] Rom. vi. 1-11, Col. ii. 10-13.

[25] I Cor. i. 13-17.

[26] I Cor. x. 1-11.

[27] Rom. vi. 12-14.

[28] Gal. vi. 14, Phil. iii. 7-11.

[29] II Cor. iv. 7-11.

[30] Col. iii. 1-4.

[31] H. G. Wells, *The New Machiavelli*, pp. 291-292.

[32] Longfellow, *Saga of King Olaf*, xxii.

THE LORD THE SPIRIT

[1] Rom. v. 8-10.

[2] Gal. v. 22-23, vi. 8, Rom. viii. 23, II Cor. i. 22, v. 5, Eph. i. 14, Col. i. 27.

[3] The *locus classicus* for "pneumatic" phenomena is I Cor. xii.-xiv., which elucidates the references to similar phenomena in Acts.

[4] II Cor. iii. 17. Instead of multiplying references to show the identity of Christ's work with that of the Spirit, I

would suggest to the interested reader that he should take a Concordance and discover for himself how often a statement made about Christ in one place can be confronted with a closely similar statement made in another place about the Spirit. He should have no difficulty in filling a quarto sheet with such doublets.

⁵ II Cor. xii. 1-9, Ac. xvi. 6-7, cf. I Cor. ii. 16, Gal. i. 12.

⁶ Thomas Hardy, *The Dynasts.*

⁷ Phil. i. 21, Gal. ii. 20, iv. 19, II Cor. iii. 12-18, Rom. xiii. 14, Eph. iii. 17. Cf. I Thess. i. 6, I Cor. xi. 1.

⁸ I Cor. xii. 13, cf. Gal. iii. 27, Rom. vi. 3.

⁹ Gal. iv. 6-7, Rom. viii. 14-17, I Cor. i. 9, Rom. viii. 26-27, Eph. vi. 18.

¹⁰ Rom. i. 19-21.

¹¹ I Cor. ii., xii. 8, II Cor. x. 3-6, I Thess. i. 5, Phil. i. 9-10, Col. ii. 2-3, Eph. i. 17, I Cor. viii. 1-3, Gal. iv. 9, I Cor. xiii. 12.

¹² Rom. ix. 1, I Cor. viii. 12.

¹³ I Cor. ii. 15, iv. 3-5.

¹⁴ See especially Phil. iii. 15-16, which a false reading represented by the A.V. has changed into a plea for uniformity!

¹⁵ Rom. xiii. 1, 4; I Cor. iv. 3.

¹⁶ Phil. iv. 13, Eph. iii. 14-19, I Cor. i. 18, 24, iv. 20, Rom. i. 16, II Cor. xii. 9-10, xiii. 3-4.

¹⁷ II Cor. v. 17 (cf. I Cor. iv. 15), Eph. ii. 10, iv. 24, Col. iii. 9-11, Rom. xii. 2.

THE DIVINE COMMONWEALTH DISCOVERED

¹ I Cor. xii., Rom. xii. 4-5, Eph. iv. 1-16, Col. i. 18-29.

² Gal. iii. 26-28, Col. iii. 11, I Cor. xii. 13.

³ The following passages will illustrate the significance of κοινωνία : II Cor. i. 7, cf. Phil. iii. 10 and Rom. viii. 17; Phm. 6, cf. 17; I Cor. x. 16-21; I Cor. i. 9, II Cor. xiii. 13; Phil. ii. 1.

⁴ I Cor. xii. 4-11, 28-31, xiv. 1-5, Rom. xii. 6-8, Eph. iv. 7-16.

⁵ Col. iii. 14-15, Rom. v. 5, Gal. v. 6.

⁶ Rom. xiii. 8-10, Gal. v. 13-14, vi. 2.

⁷ I Cor. viii. 1, cf. Eph. iv. 16.

⁸ I Cor. x. 16-21, xi. 17-34.

[9] I Cor. i. 2, x. 32, xi. 22, xv. 9, II Cor. i. 1, Gal. i. 13; cf. Gal. vi. 16.

[10] Phil. ii. 5: that this, rather than the common translation, correctly renders the Greek original, I am convinced.

THE LIFE OF THE DIVINE COMMONWEALTH

[1] Rom. xi. 33, xii. 2.

[2] II Cor. x. 1, Gal. vi. 2, Col. iii. 17.

[3] Rom. i. 24-32, I Cor. v. 10-11, II Cor. xii. 20, Gal. v. 19-21, Col. iii. 5-8.

[4] Col. ii. 16-23, I Cor. iii. 21-23, x. 23-26.

[5] Col. iii. 5 sqq.

[6] I Cor. ix.

[7] I have ventured to make Paul speak the language of Francis: neither, I think, would object!

[8] I Tim. iv. 3.

[9] I Cor. vii.

[10] Gal. iii. 28, Eph. v. 21-33, I Cor. vii. 10-11.

[11] I Thess. iv. 7-12.

[12] Lk. xii. 57.

[13] Gal. v. 22-23.

[14] Eph. iv. 25, vi. 9, Col. iii. 5, iv. 6 goes over much the same ground.

[15] *Enchiridion,* xii. 1.

[16] I Thess. v. 14.

[17] Rom. xii. 4-8.

[18] Rom. xv. 26-27.

[19] Eph. iv. 28.

[20] Preface to *Androcles and the Lion.*

[21] Acts x. 11-14. The teaching of Jesus in Mk. vii. 14-15 had evidently not been assimilated. The following verses in Mk. may represent (by a device he adopts elsewhere), under the form of a private explanation, the process by which the early Christians came to understand the meaning of their Master's teaching upon this point.

[22] I Cor. viii. 1-13, x. 14-31. In the opening of the discussion, the words "We know that we all have knowledge," and "we know that an idol is nothing in the world," are probably to be taken as citations from the letter of the Corinthian church to Paul, expressing the view of the "strong-

minded" or ultra-Pauline party. Paul accepts both statements with qualifications.

[23] Rom. xiv. 1, xv. 6.
[24] Rom. xii. 17, I Cor. x. 32, I Thess. iv. 12, cf. Col. iv. 5.
[25] Gal. vi. 10, I Thess. v. 15, Rom. i. 14, cf. xiii. 8.
[26] Rom. xiii. 1-10.
[27] Rom. xii. 14-21.
[28] Phil. ii. 15-16.
[29] Eph. ii. 19-22, iv. 12-16, i. 10, cf. Col. i. 20; I Cor. xv. 25-28.

APPENDIX

[1] First published in *The Student Movement*, 1919.

INDEX OF REFERENCES TO THE PAULINE EPISTLES

C. H. Dodd

Charles Harold Dodd was born in England in 1884 and educated at Oxford. After studying theology at Mansfield College, he was ordained in 1912 and became minister of the Congregational Church at Warwick. From 1915 to 1930 he was Yates Lecturer in New Testament Greek and Exegesis at Mansfield College. He was a lecturer in New Testament Studies at Oxford from 1927 to 1930. At Manchester from 1930 to 1935 he was Rylands Professor of Biblical Criticism and Exegesis. He was Norris-Hulse Professor of Divinity at Cambridge from 1935 to 1949. Since then he has lectured at Columbia University, Princeton Theological Seminary, and Union Theological Seminary. His other publications include *The Gospel in the New Testament* (1926), *The Authority of the Bible* (1928), *The Bible and Its Background* (1931), *The Bible and the Greeks* (1935), *Parables of the Kingdom* (1935), *History and the Gospel* (1937), *The Bible Today* (1946), *The Coming of Christ* (1951), *Gospel and Law* (1951), *Christianity and the Reconciliation of the Nations* (1952), *The Interpretation of the Fourth Gospel* (1953), and *New Testament Studies* (1953).